DO JUSTICE

The Case for Biblical Social Justice

by
Stephen Allred

For Cheri,
who inspires me to be a better person,
and for my parents,
who have shown me how to love the truth

He has told you, O mortal, what is good;
and what does the Lord require of you
but to do justice, and to love kindness,
and to walk humbly with your God?
MICAH 6:8, NRSV

TABLE OF
CONTENTS

FOREWORD

America's Founding Fathers embarked on a great experiment in democracy. But it was a limited sort of democracy, with only white male property owners entitled to vote. African slaves became the subject of an immoral compromise: counted as three-fifths of a person for purposes of allocating Congressional representation. So much for the grand ideals of the Declaration of Independence with its lofty expressions such as, "All men are created equal and endowed by their Creator with certain inalienable rights."

Women would not be able to claim the right to vote for more than a century, and despite the promise of the Civil War amendments to the Constitution, Blacks were largely excluded from voting until passage of the Voting Rights Act in 1965, whose provisions the Supreme Court eviscerated in recent years.

Wither our grand experiment in democracy? How far have we come toward achieving its promise? What work remains to be completed? Are Americans still united in even sharing the goal of our national motto: "*E pluribus unum* – out of many, one." The public resurgence of white nationalism, expressing Christian overtones, gives one pause in answering too quickly.

And what is the role of the church in this quest to forge a single national identity out of many peoples, and to extend democracy to all? The Seventh-day Adventist Church is a uniquely American institution, albeit one that has grown to become global. We were founded in the wake of a religious revival that swept the young American nation in the 1830s and 1840s, with its enthusiasm for the expected return of Christ. In our first decades, we not only proclaimed an apocalyptic message of global urgency to prepare our hearts for the coming judgment and the return of

Christ but also were actively engaged in social causes – opposing slavery, in temperance, and in religious liberty. The original Adventist church actively practiced its prophetic function.

The Biblical prophets spoke primarily to their own time and place, calling out idolatry, moral and spiritual decline, and yes, calling for justice. This has always been one of the primary roles of the church.

By the 1920s, Adventism largely followed the lead of American fundamentalism and lost its social voice and relevance. Our apocalyptic message waffled between Chicken Little-like imaginings of imminent Sunday laws and future-focused evangelism on what we expect to happen to us someday, so we better get ready! In short, we lost our balance. And America lost a potentially valuable ally in its quest for democracy and justice.

By the 1980s, Protestant America emerged from its fundamentalist hibernation and, uniting politically with Roman Catholicism, became an increasingly powerful force in American politics. Religious leaders worked to iron out theological differences, while others crafted what amounted to a political treaty between evangelicals and Catholics known as "Evangelicals and Catholics Together: the Christian Mission in the Third Millennium." It was crafted by Richard John Neuhaus, a Catholic convert and influential editor of *First Things* magazine, and Charles Colson, the Watergate felon–turned Christian celebrity and the founder of Prison Fellowship. Its Protestant endorsers represented the cream of evangelical leadership, including Bill Bright of Campus Crusade for Christ; Mark Noll, a noted professor at Wheaton College, the flagship of evangelical academia; Pat Robertson of the 700 club, and one-time presidential aspirant; and Richard Mouw, President of Fuller Theological seminary, among others.

The document was produced in 1994 and represented both a culmination of two decades of work and the foundation for what would emerge – an increasingly powerful political bloc. Seventh-day Adventists saw in this political movement something ominous, and prophetically significant. We saw the development of the very sort of religious-political alignment consistent with our understanding of America's role in prophecy. We noted the wisdom of Ellen White, who long ago described "what the church has done whenever she has lost the grace of Christ":

> Finding herself destitute of the power of love, she has reached out for the strong arm of the state to enforce her dogmas and execute her decrees. Here is the secret of all religious laws that have ever been enacted, and the secret of all persecution from the days of Abel to our own time. Christ does not drive but draws men unto Him. The only compulsion which He employs is the constraint of love. When the church *begins to seek* for the support of secular power, it is evident that she is devoid of the power of Christ–the constraint of divine love.[1]

What was to be the Adventist response to this development? Adventist religious liberty leaders began to preach and teach and warn about the dangers of church and state coming together, but alas, many Adventist pastors and church members had tuned out while tuning in, instead, to religious and secular conservative media and imbibing the values and beliefs of the religious right. The Adventist message lost its grip on many otherwise faithful, church-attending Seventh-day Adventists.

The American church began to seek the support of secular power at least by the 1970s, but its dream of a powerful alliance between evangelical Protestants and conservative Roman Catholics came to enjoy unprecedented power with the election of 2016. Ellen White's insight was that the pursuit of secular power was a sign that the church had lost the grace of God.

Now, we find ourselves at a critical juncture in our nation's history and in the life of the Seventh-day Adventist Church. Our worst racist and xenophobic tendencies rose to the fore in American politics. As a result, the spotlight began to focus on racial

---

1 Ellen G. White, *Thoughts from the Mount of Blessing*, pp. 126–127, https://egwwritings.org.

and social injustice. What will be the Seventh-day Adventist contribution to the great American experiment in democracy? Will we studiously pursue our aloofness, in the name of "coming out of Babylon?" Will we seek to justify being "so heavenly minded that we are of little earthly good?" Or will we recover our prophetic bearings and voice and take up Micah's universal mandate to "do justice, love mercy, and walk humbly" with God? At a time when the American church has largely abandoned the grace of God in pursuit of Caesar's throne, will Adventism recover grace as the foundation, not only of our gospel message but also of our contribution to American life?

With this volume, Stephen Allred is attempting to contribute to a dialogue among Seventh-day Adventists and other Christians on some of the critical racial and social justice issues of the day. These are issues fundamental to the grand American experiment in democracy, and whether we will continue to pursue the ideal of all persons being created equal.

This dialogue is urgently needed. We won't all agree, but we need to listen to one another and respect one another's viewpoints. My own views have changed over time as I listen and learn from the experience and perspectives of others. To be alive is to grow and change.

The Church State Council is pleased to partner in promoting this volume with the author, a partner in religious liberty ministry, a colleague in providing legal services to the Adventist church and its members, and a friend. I hope you will read this book thoughtfully and prayerfully. Perhaps, use it as the basis of a discussion group. Ask yourself and your own church congregation about your influence in your community. What are some practical ways you can work for justice where you live? What are your experiences with respect to racial differences? And if you are white, have you ever asked a Black friend to share their perspective? Their experience?

Our opinions suffer a great deal from a common flaw: we don't know what we don't know. So we too readily assume our opinions are well formed, based on fact and reality. They may be sound opinions based on the information that sustains them. But what happens when new information is added to the equation? New experiences?

As Christians, our faith is established upon the Word of God, and upon the unchanging Rock that is the person and character of our Savior, Jesus Christ. Because we are secure in our faith, we can accept that we know only in part and will not know fully until we are reunited with Him. Because of our faith, we can be humble about what we know, and about how much we don't know.

My hope and prayer are that we approach this volume with humility of mind, recognizing that none of us has arrived and that we have much to learn. And may this book contribute to a revival of a prophetic movement – a movement destined to impact our nation and world in positive ways.

Alan Reinach
Executive Director and General Counsel
Church State Council

PREFACE

I've changed my mind before, and no doubt you have as well. While we like to tell ourselves that our decisions are based on logic alone, the reality is that emotions often play a bigger role than we'd like to admit. All of us have baggage that impedes our ability to change our opinion on a topic, even when we may see evidence that points us in a new direction. We wonder what others will think of us, and we fear that our influence or position in the church or society may be endangered if we embrace a new or controversial idea.

I think back to my teenage years when my parents patiently tried to re-direct me away from some erroneous theological views I had picked up. Ultimately, it wasn't information alone that nudged me into the right path – it was people who showed me love and patience.

What is clear is that God is patient with us, "not wanting anyone to perish, but everyone to come to repentance" (2 Peter 3:9, NIV), and that He often leads us along gradually to understand and accept His truth. The wise man described the gradual dawning of truth as being like "the morning sun, shining ever brighter till the full light of day" (Proverbs 4:18, NIV). Sometimes, though, God sends His prophets and messengers to startle us and give us a message that will wake us up from our spiritual slumber. "Shout it aloud, do not hold back," God told Isaiah. "Raise your voice like a trumpet. Declare to my people their rebellion" (Isaiah 58:1, NIV).

In the wake of America's bloody Civil War, Ellen G. White wrote a series of articles in *The Review and Herald* where she boldly entreated church members to help the recently enslaved Black

Americans. Racist ideas were deeply entrenched in American culture; apparently with this in mind, White wrote the following:

> The opinions we have received through listening to the traditions of men must not be permitted to bar the way so that we shall not receive the light that requires reformation and transformation. Enter your closets with the Bible in your hand, and there commune with God, having an ear to hear what the Spirit saith unto you. Let your heart be humbled and teachable, softened and subdued by the Holy Spirit. If you find that your former views are not sustained by the Bible, it is for your eternal interest to learn this as soon as possible; for when God speaks in His Word, our preconceived opinions must be yielded up and our ideas brought into harmony with a "Thus saith the Lord." Christ said, "Sanctify them through thy truth; thy word is truth." With submissive spirit, you are to obey the truth at any cost, knowing that the precepts of the Bible are the word of the eternal God.[2]

There's a good chance that you will disagree with some of what you're about to read. I have done my best to apply biblical principles to the issues we discuss in the following pages, but there's also a possibility that I've missed something here or there and gotten it wrong. Nevertheless, I invite you to say a simple prayer as you start this book: "Lord, open my mind to understand and my heart to receive your truth as revealed in Scripture."

Biblical social justice is a broad term, and in this short volume we explore only a few of the myriad social justice issues addressed in Scripture and facing our society today. However, my hope and prayer is that the biblical principles we examine here will be the foundation for a discussion that will change hearts and minds – and, ultimately, lead to the pursuit of justice for the oppressed, no matter where they are found.

---

2 Ellen G. White, *The Southern Work*, p. 47, https://egwwritings.org.

A NOTE ON SOURCES

Ellen G. White (1827–1915), an advocate of biblical justice and co-founder of the Seventh-day Adventist Church, was a woman with a message. Her public speaking and voluminous writings pointed people to Jesus, emphasized God's love, encouraged people to live the golden rule, and reminded people that the test of all truth is and always will be the Bible. She spoke out on the social issues of her day, including slavery, the temperance movement, and church and state. Many consider White's ministry to have been inspired by God, noting the promise of Acts 2:17: "In the last days, God says, I will pour out my Spirit on all people. Your sons and daughters will prophesy, your young men will see visions, your old men will dream dreams" (NIV). Although she never claimed the title of "prophet," White called herself a messenger, claiming to have received dreams and visions with messages from God for His people. Sola scriptura is the foundation for the Christian faith, and it is my intention to support every important proposition made in this book with the Bible. White's writings are frequently quoted here, not as a replacement for the authority of the Bible but rather to provide valuable insight on the issues we explore. Keep reading, and I think you'll agree that the wisdom found in what she wrote about faith and social justice is an important contribution to this discussion.

"So in everything, do to others what you would have them do to you, for this sums up the Law and the Prophets"

MATTHEW 7:12, NIV

CHAPTER ONE
BIBLICAL SOCIAL JUSTICE AND POLITICAL ENGAGEMENT

It was the summer of 1963 and the height of the Civil Rights Movement in the United States. Martin Luther King Jr., a thirty-four-year-old Baptist minister, was speaking at the March on Washington for Jobs and Freedom. Over 250,000 people packed the National Mall as King delivered his "I Have a Dream" speech that has since become one of the most famous speeches of all time. With the nation listening, King proclaimed his dream that Black Americans could be equal before the law and have the same social and economic opportunities as every other American.

It had been nearly 100 years since the official end of American slavery, and yet Black Americans were still not free. The Confederacy had simply morphed into a racial caste system known as Jim Crow – a structure of laws, social norms, and mob violence aimed at keeping Blacks subjugated to the white majority in America.

On the steps of the Lincoln Memorial, King eloquently laid out the disturbing facts:

One hundred years later, the life of the Negro is still sadly crippled by the manacle of segregation and the chain of discrimination. One hundred years later, the Negro lives on a lonely island of poverty in the midst of a vast ocean of material prosperity. One hundred years later, the Negro is still languishing in the corner of American society and finds himself an exile in his own land.[3]

Today, decades after King's memorable speech, we celebrate his legacy and even have a national holiday named after him. Yet, many Americans are ignorant of King's views on social justice and what he stood for. To his contemporary critics, King was a Marxist and a socialist, and it's certain that if King were alive today, his views on social justice would still be controversial.

BIBLICAL SOCIAL JUSTICE

At the most basic level, the goal of social justice is simple: to pursue what is just and right for all members of society, especially the powerless and marginalized. But today, the term *social justice* is controversial because we often attach other meanings to it. What does the Bible have to say about social justice – does it speak to how a just society ought to function? In fact, it does. The Bible is replete with commands, stories, and admonitions about how to relate to one another in a fair, just, and equitable manner. Our goal here is to understand *biblical* social justice, and we will attempt to do so by extracting principles from the Bible that can apply to our world today.

The word often translated as *justice* in the Old Testament comes from the Hebrew word *tzedeq*, a word that also means *righteousness*. For Christians, then, justice in the context of our social and community relationships takes on an even more vital meaning. Jesus, in fact, told us that the essence of what it means to follow Him – to live a righteous life – can be summed up by our unselfish treatment of those around us. "So in everything, do to others what you would have them do to you, for this sums up the Law and the Prophets" (Matthew 7:12, NIV).

---

3 https://www.mtholyoke.edu/acad/intrel/speech/dream.htm.

Let that sink in! According to Jesus, the "law and the prophets" – essentially all of Scripture – can be boiled down to one axiom: *do to others what you would have them do to you.* Elsewhere, Jesus taught that all the law and the prophets hang on the two great commands to "love the Lord your God with all your heart" and to "love your neighbor as yourself" (Matthew 22:37–40, NIV). In fact, the Bible teaches that it is impossible to love God if we don't practice love toward our neighbor. "Those who say, 'I love God,' and hate their brothers or sisters, are liars; for those who do not love a brother or sister whom they have seen, cannot love God whom they have not seen" (1 John 4:20, NRSV). Salvation is by grace alone, and love for God and our neighbor is a fruit of God's work of grace. Living by the golden rule, then, is *prima facie* evidence that someone has been saved by God's free grace, for "everyone who loves is born of God and knows God" (1 John 4:7, NRSV). If other-centered love is the essence of the Christian life, then we ought to pay special attention to issues of societal injustice.

For Christians, social justice is applied in at least two important ways. First, there is the role of civil government in ensuring justice for the oppressed, and second, but more important, is the role of the church and the individual Christian in doing justice. Ultimately, biblical social justice is more than merely enacting laws to protect the vulnerable in society; for the believer, doing justice is about living by a principle of unselfish love. Christians also realize that earthly politics and government are not the ultimate solutions to the world's problems – Jesus is. Thus, the foremost goal for Christians is to share the gospel of God's grace with a world in need so that righteousness and justice will take root in people's hearts, and the coming kingdom of God will be hastened.

JUSTICE FOR THE MARGINALIZED

Running throughout Scripture is the pervasive theme of God's call to do justice for the oppressed. In fact, there are hundreds of Bible verses that call our attention to God's care for the poor, oppressed, widows, fatherless, immigrants, and foreigners.

For example, God warned Israel against mistreating the marginalized and powerless: "Cursed be anyone who perverts the justice due to the sojourner, the fatherless, and the widow" (Deuteronomy 27:19, ESV).

He commanded the poor to be treated fairly: "Do not deny justice to your poor people in their lawsuits. Have nothing to do with a false charge and do not put an innocent or honest person to death, for I will not acquit the guilty" (Exodus 23:6–7, NIV).

God commanded that debts were to be forgiven every seven years: "At the end of every seven years you must cancel debts. This is how it is to be done: Every creditor shall cancel any loan they have made to a fellow Israelite. They shall not require payment from anyone among their own people, because the Lord's time for canceling debts has been proclaimed" (Deuteronomy 15:1–2, NIV).

God prohibited charging interest to the poor:

If any of your fellow Israelites become poor and are unable to support themselves among you, help them as you would a foreigner and stranger, so they can continue to live among you. Do not take interest or any profit from them, but fear your God, so that they may continue to live among you. You must not lend them money at interest or sell them food at a profit. I am the Lord your God, who brought you out of Egypt to give you the land of Canaan and to be your God (Leviticus 25:35–38, NIV).

God commanded that the poor were to be allowed to harvest the fields every seventh year:

For six years you are to sow your fields and harvest the crops, but during the seventh year let the land lie unplowed and unused. Then the poor among your people may get food from it, and the wild animals may eat what is left. Do the same with your vineyard and your olive grove (Exodus 23:10–11, NIV).

God claimed ownership of the land and commanded that all land was to be returned to the family of its original owner every fifty years: "Consecrate the fiftieth year and proclaim liberty throughout the land to all its inhabitants. It shall be a jubilee for you; each of you is to return to your family property and to your own clan" (Leviticus 25:10, NIV).

And these are only a few of the examples in Scripture of how God showed His concern for the marginalized of society – the poor, oppressed, immigrants, orphans, and widows. But how are these Old Testament admonitions related to our secular world today? As we no longer live under the theocracy of ancient Israel, is it permissible for secular civil governments to extract principles from these ancient laws to be legislated today? We'll try to answer that question when we tackle the topic of economic justice in Chapter 4.

In her devotional classic, *Thoughts from the Mount of Blessing*, Ellen G. White, who advocated for the abolition of slavery in the nineteenth century and wrote extensively about poverty and human rights, made a startling statement about how biblical social justice must be a part of our religious experience:

The standard of the golden rule is the true standard of Christianity; anything short of it is a deception. A religion that leads men to place a low estimate upon human beings, whom Christ has esteemed of such value as to give Himself for them; a religion that would lead us to be careless of human needs, sufferings, or rights, is a spurious religion. In slighting the claims of the poor, the suffering, and the sinful, we are proving ourselves traitors to Christ…Search heaven and earth, and there is no truth revealed more powerful than that which is made manifest in works of mercy to those who need our sympathy and aid. This is the truth as it is in Jesus. When those who profess the name of Christ shall practice the principles of the golden rule, the same power will attend the gospel as in apostolic times.[4]

SHOULDN'T CHRISTIANS AVOID POLITICS?

It seems like every issue has become a political issue, and social justice issues are certainly no exception! As followers of Jesus, we follow a King whose kingdom is not of this world (John 18:36). As subjects of that kingdom, our first allegiance is to a heavenly country (Ephesians 2:19; Hebrews 11:16). Does that mean that we should completely disengage from any participation in the kingdoms of this world? Not necessarily.

On one hand, White warned against involvement in politics, writing the following:

> God's people have been called out of the world, that they may be separated from the world. It is not safe for them to take sides in politics, whatever preferences they may have…We are entirely out of our place when we identify ourselves with party interests. Let us not forget that we are citizens of the kingdom of heaven. We are soldiers of the cross of Christ, and our work is to advance the interests of His kingdom…[5] The Lord would have His people bury political questions. On these themes silence is eloquence.[6]

White reminds us that no matter our national allegiance or political preference, we are first and foremost citizens of the kingdom of God. As such, when the principles of the kingdoms of this world come in conflict with the principles of the kingdom of God, "we must obey God rather than men" (Acts 5:29, ESV).

---

4 Ellen G. White, *Thoughts from the Mount of Blessing*, pp. 136–137.

5 Ellen G. White, *Manuscript 67*, 1900, par. 33, https://egwwritings.org.

6 Ellen G. White, *Counsels for the Church*, p. 316, https://egwwritings.org.

Along similar lines, White pointed out that Jesus "attempted no civil reforms. He attacked no national abuses, nor condemned the national enemies. He did not interfere with the authority or administration of those in power. He who was our example kept aloof from earthly governments."[7] Some have concluded from this statement that White was opposed to any kind of involvement in social or political issues. But, as Nicholas P. Miller points out,

> those who quote this passage as defining all Adventist involvement in public matters overlook the context of the quote. It had to do with a movement we call today Christian Dominionism – believers who seek to establish a theocracy in this world...In describing Christ as keeping "aloof" from earthly governments, Ellen White was highlighting the spiritual mission of the church; but she was not purporting to set out Christians' role and duty as citizens of this world. Elsewhere she dealt with the topic of the Christian's role in public morality by word and action. In doing so, she revealed that the gospel and conversion would necessarily lead to the support of public justice, human equality, and social morality.[8]

As Miller notes, while citizens of heaven, followers of Jesus are also part of the human family who are called to do justice in the world in which they live. In realization of this fact, leaders of the early Seventh-day Adventist Church advocated for certain political issues, including the abolition of slavery, opposition to Southern secession, and the prohibition of alcohol. In 1865, after Abraham Lincoln's assassination, the newly organized General Conference of Seventh-day Adventists voted the following resolution:

> *Resolved*, That in our judgment, the act of voting when exercised in behalf of justice, humanity and right, is in itself blameless, and may be at some times highly proper; but that

---

7 Ellen G. White, *The Desire of Ages*, p. 509, https://egwwritings.org.
8 Nicholas P. Miller, *After the Dust Settles*, https://www.adventistreview.org/2101-46#disqus_thread.

the casting of any vote that shall strengthen the cause of such crimes as intemperance, insurrection, and slavery, we regard as highly criminal in the sight of Heaven. But we would deprecate any participation in the spirit of party strife.[9]

In 1880, a church member in Woodland, California, wrote to White complaining about an article published in a church publication *The Review and Herald*. In the offending article, the editor had spoken out against the evils of racism. White replied:

If our pens and voices are to be silent when principles of justice and righteousness in warnings or reproofs [are at stake] because some one or ones, believers or unbelievers, are so sensitive, bigoted, and prejudiced, that their peculiar, political sentiments cannot be in any manner referred to, that class will have to be thoroughly converted to God – their sentiments reformed.[10]

In other words, White believed that Christians should speak out about issues of "justice and righteousness," even when doing so might be perceived as being "political."

White would later encourage Christians to do something overtly political: she told them to exercise their right to vote. In 1914, she wrote: "In our favored land, every voter has some voice in determining what laws shall control the nation. Should not that influence and that vote be cast on the side of temperance and virtue?"[11]

So how do we reconcile the two apparently contradictory concepts found in White's statements above – one telling us to avoid politics and the other telling us to engage with politics by voting

---

9 "Report of the Third Annual Session of the General Conference of S.D. Adventists," *The Review and Herald*, (May 23, 1865), p. 197.

10 Ellen G. White, *Letter 36, 1880,* par. 2, https://egwwritings.org. The entire letter is included in Appendix A.

11 Ellen G. White, "The Temperance Work," *The Review and Herald*, (October 15, 1914), par. 21. See Gospel Workers, pp. 387–388, https://egwwritings.org.

and speaking out when principles of justice and righteousness are at stake?

Here are some principles to guide us:

PRINCIPLE #1:
We should avoid dabbling in partisan politics and expressing mere "political preferences" when doing so does not promote "justice and righteousness" and only creates unnecessary division.

"Watch out for people who cause divisions and upset people's faith by teaching things contrary to what you have been taught. Stay away from them. Such people are not serving Christ our Lord; they are serving their own personal interests. By smooth talk and glowing words they deceive innocent people" (Romans 16:17–18, NLT).

"You are jealous of one another and quarrel with each other. Doesn't that prove you are controlled by your sinful nature? Aren't you living like people of the world? When one of you says, 'I am a follower of Paul,' and another says, 'I follow Apollos,' aren't you acting just like people of the world?… So don't boast about following a particular human leader" (1 Corinthians 3:3–4, 21, NLT).

"The Lord would have His people bury political questions. On these themes silence is eloquence."[12]

"We cannot with safety vote for political parties; for we do not know whom we are voting for. We cannot with safety take part in any political scheme. We cannot labor to please men who will

---

12 Ellen G. White, *Counsels for the Church*, p. 316.

use their influence to repress religious liberty, and to set in operation oppressive measures to lead or compel their fellow-men to keep Sunday as the Sabbath."[13]

PRINCIPLE #2:

We should love and pray for our enemies – even our political enemies!

"I tell you, love your enemies and pray for those who persecute you" (Matthew 5:44, NIV). Keep in mind that to love one's enemies does not contradict God's command to "shout it aloud…declare to my people their rebellion" (Isaiah 58:1, NIV), or to stand up against those same enemies and "defend the rights of the poor and needy" (Proverbs 31:9, NIV). God's command to "love your enemies and pray for those who persecute you" is an invitation to participate in the character of God, who loves us even though we were His enemies (Romans 5:10), and to remember that our enemies are God's children too.

Loving someone doesn't mean we need to agree with them, but even when we disagree, Paul tells us this: "I urge, then, first of all, that petitions, prayers, intercession and thanksgiving be made for all people – for kings and all those in authority" (1 Timothy 2:1–2, NIV).

---

13 Ellen G. White, *Gospel Workers*, p. 391, https://egwwritings.org.

PRINCIPLE #3:

**We should avoid condemning individuals
– even politicians we dislike. Yet, we may be called
to "speak truth to power."**

"Be wise in the way you act toward outsiders; make the most
of every opportunity. Let your conversation be always full of
grace, seasoned with salt, so that you may know how to answer
everyone" (Colossians 4:5–6, NIV).

"The less we make direct charges against authorities and
powers, the greater work we shall be able to accomplish…
If we wish men to be convinced that the truth we believe
sanctifies the soul and transforms the character, let us not be
continually charging them with vehement accusations. In this
way we shall force them to the conclusion that the doctrine
we profess cannot be the Christian doctrine, since it does not
make us kind, courteous, and respectful. Christianity is not
manifested in pugilistic accusations and condemnation."[14]

Like John the Baptist, who "rebuked Herod the tetrarch
because of his marriage to Herodias, his brother's wife, and all
the other evil things he had done," (Luke 3:19, NIV), we may
be called to speak truth to power. However, we will do it in love.
Afterall, even Nebuchadnezzar, the pagan king of Babylon,
eventually gave his heart to God.

---

14 Ellen G. White, *Testimonies for the Church*, vol. 6, pp. 395–397, https://egwwritings.org.

PRINCIPLE #4:
Christians can legitimately assert their civil rights.

While Christ's followers are called to submit to earthly governments to the extent that the laws of the land do not violate God's law (Romans 13; Acts 5:28–29) and to suffer persecution quietly (1 Peter 4:13–15), nonetheless, there is nothing wrong with Christians asserting their civil rights when that glorifies God or promotes justice for the oppressed (Acts 16:37; 22:26; Proverbs 31:8–9). Paul and Silas asserted their civil rights under Roman law and insisted that the political leaders who had unjustly imprisoned them publicly demonstrate their support for their release from jail (Acts 16:35–39). And Christians may even be called to exercise civil disobedience when a law violates the higher law of God (Acts 5:29).

PRINCIPLE #5:
**Christians have a moral responsibility
to use their voice and vote to advocate for justice
and righteousness on behalf of the oppressed – even
when doing so may involve political engagement.**

The wise man wrote: "Speak up for those who cannot speak for themselves, for the rights of all who are destitute. Speak up and judge fairly; defend the rights of the poor and needy" (Proverbs 31:8–9, NIV).

The Hebrew midwives disobeyed Pharaoh's unjust law in order to save the Hebrew babies (Exodus 1:17). God used Moses to speak the truth to Pharaoh and deliver the Israelites from the oppression of Egyptian slavery. Mordecai and Esther were placed in positions of influence in the Persian empire so they could advocate for justice on behalf of the exiled Jews. The ancient Hebrew prophets spoke up on behalf of the poor, widows, orphans, and oppressed. And in one startling example of defending the rights of others, Abraham rescued his nephew Lot from his captors, showing that "righteousness is not cowardice, and that Abraham's religion made him courageous in maintaining the right and defending the oppressed."[15]

White encouraged individuals who had ambitions to serve in political office, writing: "Dear youth, what is the aim and purpose of your life? Are you ambitious for education that you may have a name and position in the world? Have you thought that you dare not express, that you may one day stand upon the summit of intellectual greatness; that you may sit in deliberative and legislative councils, and help to enact laws for the nation? *There is nothing wrong in these aspirations.* You may every one of you make your mark. You should be content with no mean attainments. Aim high, and spare no pains to reach the standard."[16]

During the Civil War, writing in her capacity as a church leader, White spoke out against slavery and the political issue of Southern secession. She rebuked a church member who supported the Confederacy, writing: "God is punishing the North, that they have so long suffered the accursed sin of slavery to exist; for in the sight of heaven it is a sin of the darkest dye. God is not with the South, and He will punish them dreadfully in the end. Satan is the instigator of all rebellion. *I saw that you, Brother A, have permitted your political principles to destroy your judgment and your love for the truth.* They are eating out true godliness from your heart. You have never looked upon slavery in the right light, and your views of this matter have thrown you on the side of the Rebellion, which was stirred up

---

15 Ellen G. White, *Patriarchs and Prophets*, p. 135, https://egwwritings.org.
16 Ellen G. White, *A Call to Stand Apart*, p. 64, https://egwwritings.org..

by Satan and his host. Your views of slavery cannot harmonize with the sacred, important truths for this time. *You must yield your views or the truth…We must let it be known that we have no such ones [sympathizers with slavery and the Confederacy] in our fellowship, that we will not walk with them in church capacity."*[17]

Decades later, White advocated for Christians to be involved in the temperance movement. *"While we are in no wise to become involved in political questions,* yet it is our privilege to take our stand decidedly on all questions relating to temperance reform…There is a cause for the moral paralysis upon society. Our laws sustain an evil which is sapping their very foundations. Many deplore the wrongs which they know exist, but consider themselves free from all responsibility in the matter. This cannot be. Every individual exerts an influence in society…*In our favored land, every voter has some voice in determining what laws shall control the nation. Should not that influence and that vote be cast on the side of temperance and virtue?…*We need not expect that God will work a miracle to bring about this reform, and thus remove the necessity for our exertion. We ourselves must grapple with this giant foe, our motto, No compromise and no cessation of our efforts till the victory is gained."[18]

Most of us understand this last principle. When White wrote these words, she was concerned with the societal issue of "temperance" (alcohol prohibition), which was a moral issue that also happened to be a political issue in her day. You can remove the word *temperance* and insert any other moral-social issue, and the same counsel could apply today.

---

17 Ellen G. White, *Testimonies for the Church*, vol. 1, pp. 359–360, https://egwwritings.org..
18 Ellen G. White, "The Temperance Work," *The Review and Herald*, (October 15, 1914), par. 16, 21–22. See Gospel Workers, pp. 387–388.

RACISM: A CASE STUDY

For example, is racism a moral issue that ought to be confronted? Martin Luther King Jr. and Ellen G. White certainly thought so. Some Christians today want to avoid dealing with racism because it's divisive *and political!* Other Christians recognize that abortion is a moral and political issue – and also an extremely divisive one. Both groups of Christians have no problem advocating for their views. And both groups ought to recognize that both abortion and racism – as well as many other social issues – should concern followers of Jesus.

Douglas Morgan observes that White did not believe that Christians should be involved in using "politics as instrument of power and control." But she did believe that Christians are justified in being involved in politics as a means of "exposing tyranny and political iniquity, speaking out with forceful clarity on issues of justice and mercy."[19]

Morgan succinctly summarizes White's position on engagement with politics:

Two guideposts from Ellen White's counsel thus come into sharper focus. First, those who speak under the banner of the… Church cannot "dabble in politics." The Church's message and mission require a free agency under God that must not be compromised or corrupted by entanglements with political parties or other partisan interests. Second, [Christians] should not be silent about injustice, exploitation, and inhumanity, even if advocacy for legislative or public policy changes stirs political opposition.[20]

---

19 Douglas Morgan, "Sinful Sentiments and Republican Purity – Ellen White and the Politics of Racial Justice (Part II)," *Spectrum*, https://spectrummagazine.org/news/2020/sinful-sentiments-and-republican-purity-ellen-white-and-politics-racial-justice-part-ii.
20 Ibid.

JESUS, NOT POLITICS, IS OUR ULTIMATE HOPE

Even while we should care about advancing justice through laws, we cannot let it eclipse our most important job of sharing the everlasting gospel. The gospel of God's grace is the ultimate solution to injustice in our world:

> The only remedy for the sins and sorrows of men is Christ. The gospel of His grace alone can cure the evils that curse society. *The injustice of the rich toward the poor, the hatred of the poor toward the rich, alike have their root in selfishness, and this can be eradicated only through submission to Christ.* He alone, for the selfish heart of sin, gives the new heart of love. Let the servants of Christ preach the gospel with the Spirit sent down from heaven, and work as He did for the benefit of men. Then such results will be manifest in the blessing and uplifting of mankind as are wholly impossible of accomplishment by human power.[21]

Jesus is the remedy.

The gospel of His grace is the cure.

Which doesn't mean, of course, that we should fold our hands and do nothing to make the world a better place in other ways as well. In the words of White, "every voter has some voice in determining what laws shall control the nation. Should not that influence and that vote be cast on the side of temperance and virtue?"[22]

But White reminds us that while we vote and work for societal change, Jesus has the ultimate answers to the world's problems. It was Jesus, after all, who summed up both our spiritual *and social duty* in this simple, yet life-changing, maxim: "Do to others what you would have them do to you" (Matthew 7:12, NIV).

---

21 Ellen G. White, *Christ's Object Lessons,* p. 254.
22 Ellen G. White, "The Temperance Work," *The Review and Herald,* (October 15, 1914), par. 21.

TAKE ACTION: DO JUSTICE NOW

• Knowing what the Bible says about social justice, how can I do justice in the world?

• Who in my family, workplace, or social circle needs help that I can give?

• How can I step outside of my circle and help those in need who are different from me?

*"For this is the message you
heard from the beginning:
We should love one another.
Do not be like Cain, who
belonged to the evil one
and murdered his brother"*

1 JOHN 3:11-12, NIV

CHAPTER TWO
MY BROTHER'S KEEPER?

"Where is your brother?" The question hung in the air as the blood of the world's first murder victim was still on the hands of the world's first murderer. In response to God's query, Cain deflected and tried to absolve himself of responsibility. "I don't know," he replied. "Am I my brother's keeper?" (Genesis 4:9, NIV).

In a way, our world is still asking the same question: *To what extent do I have to look out for the welfare of other people?*

There are two apparently contradictory concepts in Scripture. On the one hand, there is the concept that we are not guilty for the sins of our parents. The prophet Ezekiel speaks of those who receive God's righteousness and repent of their sins: "The one who sins is the one who will die. The child will not share the guilt of the parent, nor will the parent share the guilt of the child" (Ezekiel 18:20, NIV). On the other hand, there is the idea of corporate responsibility woven throughout Scripture.

First, the Bible teaches that when we continue in our parents' sins, to which we are naturally inclined, we also partake in their guilt (See, e.g., Exodus 20:5–6; Matthew 23:34–36). Second, the Bible teaches that we, as members of society, share a collective responsibility to love and care for our neighbors. We are repeatedly commanded in Scripture to love our neighbor as ourselves, with the Apostle Paul telling us that "all the law is fulfilled in one word, even in this; Thou shalt love thy neighbor as thyself" (Galatians 5:14, KJV). This debt of love to our neighbor includes the command to "defend the rights" of the oppressed and to seek justice for the mistreated. (See, e.g., Romans 13:8 and Proverbs 31:8–9.)

There is a strange story found in 2 Samuel 21 that illustrates how seriously God considers the mistreatment of the oppressed and our collective responsibility to make sure they are treated right. "Now there was a famine in the days of David for three years, year after year. And David sought the face of the Lord. And the Lord said, 'There is bloodguilt on Saul and on his house, because he put the Gibeonites to death'" (2 Samuel 21:1, ESV).

Notice what's happening here:

- There was a famine in the land of Israel, and everyone in Israel was suffering as a result.

- David prays and God responds by telling David there is sin in the camp. Years earlier, Saul and his family had committed atrocities against the Gibeonites, an ethnic minority in the land of Israel.

- Centuries before that, Israel's leaders had sworn to the Gibeonites that they would not be killed, and Saul had broken that oath.

- Saul is now gone, and David is the king. Whether David knew of Saul's actions or not, he and all Israel are suffering nonetheless.

- Even though David had nothing to do with Saul's sin, he understands it is his job to make restitution to the Gibeonites.

How does David respond to the situation? "And David said to the Gibeonites, 'What shall I do for you? And how shall I make atonement, that you may bless the heritage of the Lord?'" (2 Samuel 21:3, ESV).

Notice how honestly and forthrightly King David confronted the issue. First, he "sought the Lord" to ascertain the cause of the famine. Once he discovered the answer, he didn't tell the

Gibeonites, "It's not my fault; get over it." Instead, he asked, "What can I do to make this right?"

This Bible story fits with the overall biblical narrative that we as human beings owe a debt of love to each other and that we ought to defend the oppressed. (See, e.g., Romans 13:8 and Proverbs 31:8–9.) This story also suggests that we have a collective responsibility to, as far as possible, rectify the wrongs of our society – even the wrongs committed by our ancestors that still affect those around us today.

The story of Achan, in Joshua 7, is another biblical example of corporate responsibility. The Bible says that "*the children of Israel committed a trespass* regarding the accursed things, for Achan the son of Carmi, the son of Zabdi, the son of Zerah, of the tribe of Judah, took of the accursed things; so the anger of the Lord burned against the children of Israel" (Joshua 7:1, NKJV).

There's no question that Achan was the one who had taken the prohibited goods from Jericho and sinned. Yet, the Bible indicates that the whole Israelite nation was somehow involved in committing the sin: "When Achan son of Zerah was unfaithful in regard to the devoted things, did not wrath come on the whole community of Israel? He was not the only one who died for his sin." (Joshua 22:20, NIV). White observed that "the nation was held accountable for the guilt of the transgressor."[23] Additionally, Achan's entire family perished with him, even though there is no record that they had directly participated in his sin. Timothy Keller notes that

Achan's family…did not do the stealing, but they helped him become the kind of man who would steal. The Bible's emphasis on the importance of the family for character

---

23 Ellen G. White, *Patriarchs and Prophets*, p. 494, https://egwwritings.org.

formation implies that the rest of the family cannot wholly avoid responsibility for the behavior of a member.[24]

None other than Jesus Himself taught us the truth of corporate responsibility when He told the Pharisees that by persecuting Him and His followers, they were actually participating in the sins of those who had killed the prophets centuries before.

Therefore, I am sending you prophets and sages and teachers. Some of them you will kill and crucify; others you will flog in your synagogues and pursue from town to town. *And so upon you will come all the righteous blood that has been shed on earth,* from the blood of righteous Abel to the blood of Zechariah son of Berekiah, whom you murdered between the temple and the altar. Truly I tell you, all this will come on this generation (Matthew 23:34–36, NIV).

Strikingly, Jesus attributed the guilt of Zechariah's murder, hundreds of years earlier, to the religious leaders of His day. *In other words, it's possible to participate in the guilt of our ancestors when we partake of the same spirit that motivated them, or commit, to a greater or lesser degree, the same sins that they committed.* Which is what the Bible seems to be getting at when God describes Himself as "a jealous God, punishing the children for the sin of the parents to the third and fourth generation of those who hate me, but showing love to a thousand generations of those who love me and keep my commandments" (Exodus 20:5–6, NIV).

In 1 Samuel 15, the prophet Samuel delivered a message to King Saul: "This is what the Lord Almighty says: 'I will punish the Amalekites for what they did to Israel when they waylaid them as they came up from Egypt. Now go, attack the Amalekites and totally destroy all that belongs to them'" (1 Samuel 15:2–3, NIV). Approximately 400 years had passed since the Amalekites

---

24 Timothy Keller, A Biblical Critique of Secular Justice and Critical Theory, https://quarterly. gospelinlife.com/a-biblical-critique-of-secular-justice-and-critical-theory/.

had attacked the Israelites on their way out of Egypt. Neverthe-less, Saul was commanded to destroy the descendants of these same Amalekites. Why was this? Simply put, the Amalekites of Saul's day had the same attitudes and character qualities as did their ancestors centuries before. By participating in the same sins, they also participated in their ancestors' guilt.

> By divine direction the history of their cruelty toward Israel had been recorded, with the command, "Thou shalt blot out the remembrance of Amalek from under heaven; thou shalt not forget it." Deuteronomy 25:19. For four hundred years, the execution of this sentence had been deferred; but the Amale-kites had not turned from their sins. The Lord knew that this wicked people would, if it were possible, blot out His people and His worship from the earth. Now the time had come for the sentence, so long delayed, to be executed.[25]

Similarly, the end-time apostate religionists – represented by the imagery of the great city Babylon – are implicated in the demise of "all who have been slaughtered on the earth" (Reve-lation 18:24, NIV), even though they did not personally commit all the murders. Again, the Bible is telling us, we can be held responsible for the sins of others when we participate in those same sins through our attitudes, choices, and actions.

However, while the Bible teaches corporate responsibility, it also teaches that we are not responsible for the sins of our parents to the extent that we repudiate those sins and seek to rectify the injustices they committed. (See, e.g., Ezekiel 18:14–20; Matthew 23:37.) Keller explains how our own choices ultimately determine our eternal destiny:

> There is an asymmetrical balance between individual and corporate responsibility. Deuteronomy 24:16 says that in ordinary

---

25 Ellen G. White, *Patriarchs and Prophets*, pp. 627–628.

human law, we must be held responsible and punished for our own sins, not those of our parents. We are indeed the product of our communities, but not wholly – we can resist their patterns. Ezekiel 18 is a case study of what can happen if we put too much emphasis on corporate responsibility – it leads to "fatalism and irresponsibility." *The reality of corporate sin does not swallow up individual moral responsibility, nor does individual responsibility disprove the reality of corporate evil.* To deny (or largely deny) either is to adopt one of the secular views of justice rather than a biblical one.[26]

In other words, both individual responsibility and corporate responsibility are biblical truths that should inform how we do justice as we live our lives today.

CORPORATE RESPONSIBILITY TODAY

How can this apply to us today? One example would be the problem of racism in America – a problem that we will address in greater detail in Chapter 3.

Just over a century ago, in the dreadful wake of American slavery, and over thirty years after the Civil War had ended, Ellen White applied the biblical principle of corporate responsibility to the American nation, writing, "The neglect of the colored race by the American nation is charged against them."[27]

The American nation owes a debt of love to the colored race, and God has ordained that they should make restitution for the wrong they have done them in the past. *Those who have taken no active part in enforcing slavery upon the colored people are not relieved from the responsibility of making special efforts to remove, as far as possible, the sure result of their enslavement.*[28]

---

26 Keller, *A Biblical Critique of Secular Justice and Critical Theory*.

27 Ellen G. White, *The Southern Work*, p. 44.

28 Ellen G. White, "Am I My Brother's Keeper?" *The Review and Herald*, (January 21, 1896), par. 1.

During the same era in American history, White also indicted the church, writing that "the people who have been more favorably situated, who have had light and liberty, who have had an opportunity to know God, and Jesus Christ whom He has sent, are responsible for the moral darkness that enshrouds their colored brethren."[29] She later wrote that the "degraded condition [of American Blacks during the post-reconstruction era] is our condemnation. The Christian world are guilty because they have failed to help the very ones who most need help."[30]

It's safe to argue that the "debt of love" White wrote about in 1896 is still outstanding. Has America ever made "restitution" (a term used by Ellen White) to the slaves or their ancestors for the horrors of slavery? No. In fact, far from "making special efforts to remove, as far as possible, the sure result of their enslavement," most of America doubled down after the end of the Civil War. White supremacy and racism against Blacks became entrenched in many parts of American culture. Jim Crow laws were created and enforced with swift and lethal brutality. Black Americans were lynched for simply looking a white person in the eye or being in the wrong place at the wrong time. Even northern Yankees didn't want Blacks moving into their cities, and riots ensued. Historians sympathetic to the former Confederacy revised history to create the narrative of the "lost cause," making heroes out of the Confederate leaders and ideology. To this day, many Americans continue to idolize the Confederacy and what it stood for.

What happens to a debt that hasn't been paid or a sin that hasn't been atoned for? Does it just magically disappear? Not according to the Bible. The injustices done and the atrocities committed have not been forgotten by God. God is "compassionate and gracious…slow to anger, abounding in love and faithfulness, maintaining love to thousands, and forgiving wickedness, rebellion and sin." Yet when sin is unconfessed and unforsaken,

---

29 Ellen G. White, *The Southern Work*, pp. 31–32.
30 Ibid., p. 35.

and when the children perpetuate the sins of the parents, God declares that "he does not leave the guilty unpunished; he punishes the children and their children for the sin of the parents to the third and fourth generation" (Exodus 34:6–7, NIV).

When the leaders of Egypt refused to free the enslaved Israelites, God's judgments came upon all Egypt. The temporarily chastened Egyptians made grudging monetary restitution to the Israelites in the form of jewels, gold, and silver (Exodus 12:33–36). Other judgments fell upon the Egyptians responsible for enslaving the Israelites, as their firstborn sons died, and Pharaoh and his military forces were drowned in the Red Sea (Exodus 12:29; 14:26–28). Individual Egyptians, however, had a choice to renounce the ways of the oppressive empire, be covered with the blood of the lamb, and escape the land of slavery with the liberated Israelites (Exodus 12:38).

Millions of Black Americans alive today are direct descendants of enslaved people. Millions of Black Americans living today were alive during the era of Jim Crow, which officially ended only a few short decades ago when the Civil Rights Act of 1964 was passed. Some of the perpetrators of the racial violence of the Civil Rights era are still alive today. The effects of that mammoth system of slavery and the subsequent state-sanctioned discrimination and violence are still being felt in America today – socially, economically, and otherwise. Even if, in the words of White, we have taken "no active part in enforcing slavery," we "are not relieved from the responsibility of making special efforts to remove, as far as possible, the sure result" of that abominable system of oppression.

King David made restitution to the Gibeonites for the actions of King Saul, even though he had nothing to do with what Saul had done. Once David made things right, the famine in the land, from which all Israel suffered, ceased. Should we not be at least as forthright and proactive as was King David in seeking to bring about justice and reconciliation in our world today?

Where do we begin? The prophet Daniel gives us a starting point. Daniel confessed the sins of his people as though they were his own sins.

Lord, the great and awesome God, who keeps his covenant of love with those who love him and keep his commandments, we have sinned and done wrong. We have been wicked and have rebelled; we have turned away from your commands and laws...Now, our God, hear the prayers and petitions of your servant...We do not make requests of you because we are righteous, but because of your great mercy. Lord, listen! Lord, forgive! Lord, hear and act! (Daniel 9:4–5, 17–19, NIV).

God is full of mercy and compassion for us. It was Jesus who showed us the fullest extent of that mercy with His arms stretched out on the Roman cross beam. As the soldiers pounded the spikes through his wrists and feet, He prayed for His Father to forgive His persecutors. His prayer encompassed the entire human family – to all who will confess their sin and receive the mercy and forgiveness He offers.

TAKE ACTION: DO JUSTICE NOW

- What are some injustices I may not have directly caused or participated in that I can help remedy?

- How can I, like King David, seek to make things right in regard to those injustices I've listed above?

- How can I be like Jesus and forgive my enemies?

"Justice, and only justice,
you shall pursue, so that you
may live and occupy the land that
the Lord your God is giving you."
DEUTERONOMY 16:20, NRSV

CHAPTER THREE
AMERICA'S
ORIGINAL SIN

American Christians are as divided as ever on the subject of racism. Some believe that racism doesn't exist in America – and that acknowledging it will only create more problems. This group insists that Christians must simply unite and "focus on the gospel." Still, others have experienced racism themselves and see evidence of systemic racism in America. They believe that to follow the command of Jesus to "do unto others as you would have them do to you" requires them to seek justice for those experiencing racism. Both groups can hopefully agree on one thing: that racism is wrong. After all, "God does not show favoritism," and Jesus told His followers to take the gospel to "every nation, tribe, language and people" (Acts 10:34; Revelation 14:6, NIV).

What if someone confides in you about their abusive marriage? They tell you: "I'm married to an abusive person. The abuse isn't as bad as it used to be, but some of the abusive behavior is still there. My partner has never acknowledged that how they've treated me was wrong or tried to make it right. What should I do?" What if you tell that person: "Your marriage problems are just sin problems. The more you talk about the problems, the more you'll create division in your marriage. Don't have a victim mentality. Just try to be united with your spouse. Forget the past and focus on the good things in your marriage." Have you helped the abused partner to work through their marriage problem or merely swept it under the rug and enabled more abuse? The abusive spouse has never been held to account, never repented or formally apologized, and never made restitution for the harm they have done.

While the victim spouse needs to forgive, the abusive spouse must be lovingly but firmly held to account, and the abuse needs to stop. Even if the abusive behavior has stopped, there needs to be confession of sin and restitution. (See, e.g., Ezekiel 33:15; 2 Samuel 21:3.)

The same is true for racism in America. As Christians, we know racism is ultimately a sin problem. White Americans have historically made the color of people's skin an issue. When Black people, or other people of color, raise their voices asking for help, we can't just tell them to stop talking about racism because it's divisive. Instead, we need to listen and admit that we, as an American nation and church, have been in denial about this issue for a long time.

Ta-Nehisi Coates observes that:

> In America, there is a strange and powerful belief that if you stab a black person 10 times, the bleeding stops and the healing begins the moment the assailant drops the knife. We believe white dominance to be a fact of the inert past, a delinquent debt that can be made to disappear if only we don't look.[31]

But Ellen G. White didn't think American racism had yet been dealt with. She had no problem speaking out on this issue, even though she knew it would make some people upset. "While we will endeavor to keep the 'unity of the Spirit' in the bonds of peace," she wrote, "we will not with pen or voice cease to protest against bigotry."[32]

---

31 Ta-Nehisi Coates, "The Case for Reparations," *The Atlantic*, https://www.theatlantic.com/magazine/archive/2014/06/the-case-for-reparations/361631/?gclid=CjwKCAiA-f78BRBbEiwATKRRBPHzjH-6ChQW-N9z8eeahshZIcy6kQouJV_nYzrO5XSGQkONuPbXiiBoC81AQAvD_BwE.

32 Ellen G. White, *Last Day Events*, p. 48, https://egwwritings.org.

I know that that which I now speak will bring me into conflict. This I do not covet, for the conflict has seemed to be continuous of late years; but I do not mean to live a coward or die a coward, leaving my work undone. I must follow in my Master's footsteps. It has become fashionable to look down upon the poor, and upon the colored race in particular. But Jesus, the Master, was poor, and He sympathizes with the poor, the discarded, the oppressed, and declares that every insult shown to them is as if shown to Himself. *I am more and more surprised as I see those who claim to be children of God possessing so little of the sympathy, tenderness, and love which actuated Christ.* Would that every church, north and south, were imbued with the spirit of our Lord's teaching.[33]

THE ABOMINATION OF AMERICAN SLAVERY

A lack of knowledge may be one of the reasons many Christians are apathetic or hostile to the idea of confronting racism. Most Americans are largely ignorant of the history of racism in America. Nineteenth-century American slavery and the state-sponsored racism that followed were much worse than most schoolchildren are ever taught. "Unspeakable outrages," White wrote, "have been committed against the colored race."[34] Knowing history is necessary to not only avoid repeating its mistakes but also aid us in understanding how these events of the past still reverberate today. As Jesus-followers, we must be willing to confront this terrible past and see where the ugly racism of the human heart has led our ancestors – and where it can lead us today.

The atrocities had only begun when human beings created in God's image were loaded like cargo onto slave ships on the African coast to be transported to the Americas, where they

---

33 Ellen G. White, *The Southern Work*, pp. 10–11.
34 Ibid., p. 44.

would become fuel for the American economy. To increase profits, slavers would cram as many African men and women as possible into the hold of their ship. Stripped of clothing and confined to small, filthy spaces with little headroom, the newly enslaved were tightly chained to plank beds, where many succumbed to disease and died a terrible but merciful death on the long trip over the Atlantic Ocean. The PBS mini-series *The African Americans: Many Rivers to Cross* documents the horrors of this journey through the "Middle Passage."

Solomon Northup's graphic and harrowing nineteenth-century memoir documents his real-life experience of being kidnapped as a Black freeman in America and sold into slavery. *Twelve Years a Slave* was made into a movie a few years ago. Northup's account of slavery in North America shows that upon arrival in the New World, things only worsened for the enslaved. By law, "negroes" had no inalienable rights in the land of the free, and they were not considered people under the original United States Constitution. Enslaved men and women were nothing more than a commodity, human chattel, and the property of the white man or woman who bought them. On the slave owner's auction block, babies were torn from their mother's arms – never to be seen again. A husband might be sold to a buyer in Texas, while the wife went to a Virginia planter.

Historian Edward E. Baptist, in his book *The Half Has Never Been Told: Slavery and the Making of American Capitalism*, describes how Charles Ball, a young enslaved boy, was ripped away from his mother who had just been sold to a Georgia buyer:

A Maryland man bought the little boy and wrapped him in his own child's spare gown. Putting Charles up in front of him, the buyer turned his horse's head toward home. Before he could leave, Charles's mother came running up, weeping. She took Charles down into her arms, hugged him and pleaded through tears for the man to buy them all. She only got a moment to make her case. Down came the Georgia man, running in his heavy boots, wading into her with his whip, beating her shoulders until she handed Charles over. The Georgia buyer dragged her screaming toward the yard. The crying boy clung to the Maryland man, his new owner.[35]

As if forced separation wasn't bad enough, enslaved women were routinely raped by their white "Christian" owners; their bodies forced to submit to the brutality of the master who claimed to own them. Some masters kept lists of the scores of enslaved women they had raped, many of them young teenage girls. Thus, any semblance of family structure in the African American enslaved community was perverted and destroyed by the brutality of the white enslavers. Add to this the systematic physical torture – the brutal lashings and beatings – that many Southern plantation masters frequently inflicted on those they claimed to own, and it is not difficult to conclude that American slavery left indelible physical, mental, emotional, and spiritual scars on the enslaved and their descendants.

Ta-Nehisi Coates calls out today's critics who blame Black America's problems on the breakdown of the family, noting that

the laments about "black pathology," the criticism of black family structures by pundits and intellectuals, ring hollow in a country whose existence was predicated on the torture of black fathers, on the rape of black mothers, on the sale of black children. An honest assessment of America's relationship to the black family reveals the country to be not its nurturer but its destroyer.[36]

---

35 Edward E. Baptist, *The Half Has Never Been Told: Slavery and the Making of American Capitalism* (New York: Basic Books, 2016), p. 18.
36 Coates, "The Case for Reparations."

Of America during this time, Ellen White would write:

The people of this nation have exalted themselves to heaven, and have looked down upon monarchical governments, and triumphed in their boasted liberty, *while the institution of slavery, that was a thousand times worse than the tyranny exercised by monarchial governments, was suffered to exist and was cherished.* In this land of light a system is cherished which allows one portion of the human family to enslave another portion, degrading millions of human beings to the level of the brute creation. *The equal of this sin is not to be found in heathen lands…*God is punishing this nation for the high crime of slavery. He has the destiny of the nation in His hands. He will punish the South for the sin of slavery, and the North for so long suffering its overreaching and overbearing influence.[37]

In the same vein as White, Coates writes about how the destruction of the Black family was the foundation of "American wealth and democracy – in the for-profit destruction of the most important asset available to any people, the family." Coates notes, "The destruction was not incidental to America's rise; it facilitated that rise. By erecting a slave society, America created the economic foundation for its great experiment in democracy." Enslaved Blacks were America's original "indispensable working class," Coates argues, and they "existed as property beyond the realm of politics, leaving white Americans free to trumpet their love of freedom and democratic values."[38]

It finally took a war to officially end the abomination of race-based slavery in America. Yet many Americans today proudly celebrate the Confederacy and the "way of life" it represented, refusing to recognize or confront the problems created by the legacy of white supremacy and slavery.

---

37 Ellen G. White, *Testimonies for the Church,* vol. 1, pp. 258–259, 264.
38 Coates, "The Case for Reparations."

STATE-SPONSORED RACIAL TERROR

But widespread brutality toward Blacks in America didn't cease with the Civil War. In 1899, White wrote,

> The whites who have oppressed the colored people still have the same spirit. They did not lose it, although they were conquered in war. They are determined to make it appear that the blacks were better off in slavery than since they were set free. Any provocation from the blacks is met with the greatest cruelty.[39]

In fact, lynching – defined as the act of killing someone without a legal trial – continued with a vengeance, with over 4,000 Blacks being lynched in the South between the years 1877 and 1950 alone. The Equal Justice Initiative (EJI), a nonprofit human rights organization, describes the lynching of African Americans as "terrorism, a widely supported phenomenon used to enforce racial subordination and segregation. Lynchings were violent and public events that traumatized Black people throughout the country and were largely tolerated by state and federal officials."[40]

Why were they lynched? "Many African Americans who were never accused of any crime were tortured and murdered in front of picnicking spectators (including elected officials and prominent citizens) for bumping into a white person, or wearing their military uniforms after the First World War, or not using the appropriate title when addressing a white person." To add insult to injury, "people who participated in lynchings were celebrated and acted with impunity."[41]

---

39 Ellen G. White, *The Southern Work*, p. 83.
40 Equal Justice Initiative, "Lynching in America," https://eji.org/reports/lynching-in-america/.
41 Ibid.

THE LEGAL ROOTS OF AMERICAN RACISM

Legal history illustrates how deeply racism has been inter-woven into the laws and customs of American society. For example, Virginia was the first of the American colonies to codify the enslavement of "the negro" and others based on the color of their skin, their country of origin, or their religion. "An act concerning Servants and Slaves" was passed by the Commonwealth's General Assembly in 1705 and delineated in detail the rights that white Christian owners had over the bodies and destinies of the enslaved and their offspring. Over 150 years of legalized brutality followed, culminating with the Civil War.

When the Thirteenth Amendment was ratified in 1865, slavery officially became illegal in the United States. But while the Black man was legally free, he was not free to be the white man's equal. Far from it. Following Reconstruction, the United States Supreme Court in *Plessy v. Ferguson* (1896) upheld state imposed racial segregation – the "separate but equal" doctrine. Many whites in both the Northern and Southern United States sup-ported the Court's decision because of their belief that people with white skin were inherently superior to those with darker skin. Southern states enacted laws – known as Jim Crow or Black Code laws – that effectively relegated Blacks to the status of second-class citizens. Blacks were often incarcerated on trumped up charges and fined. When unable to pay the fines, they were required to work in chain gangs. Thus, slavery continued in another form. In the words of W.E.B. Du Bois, "The slave went free; stood for a brief moment in the sun; then moved back again toward slavery."[42]

Coates writes that

Terrorism carried the day. Federal troops withdrew from the South in 1877. The dream of Reconstruction died. For

---

[42] W.E. B. Du Bois, *Black Reconstruction in America* (New York: Simon and Schuster, 1935), p. 30.

the next century, political violence was visited upon blacks wantonly, with special treatment meted out toward black people of ambition. Black schools and churches were burned to the ground. Black voters and the political candidates who attempted to rally them were intimidated, and some were murdered. At the end of World War I, black veterans returning to their homes were assaulted for daring to wear the American uniform.[43]

Jim Crow continued in full force until only a few decades ago when the Court overturned the *Plessy* decision in *Brown v. Board of Education* (1955) and Congress passed the Civil Rights Act of 1964. Many people alive today lived through the Civil Rights Movement, when Blacks were mowed down with fire hoses, beaten by the police, terrorized by whites, and treated worse than animals.

Not long after the Civil War, during the post-reconstruction era as Jim Crow ushered in this new form of slavery, Ellen White commented somewhat cryptically:

> *Every species of slavery* is not in accordance with the Word of God. The evils are too great to be enumerated. And if men and women have embraced the solemn truth for these last days that sanctifies the soul, *the old political sentiments that sustain the old system of slavery will be, before they are translated, purged from them.*[44]

Perhaps a more subtle form of discrimination, but one with long-term effects, took the form of "red-lining," in which Blacks were prohibited from buying homes in nice parts of town or denied home loans, effectively barring them from home ownership. While the American middle class has traditionally built and transmitted wealth to their children though home ownership, many Blacks did not have the same opportunities in this area as did whites, leaving them and their descendants economically disadvantaged. Richard Rothstein in his book, *The Color of Law:*

---

43 Coates, "The Case for Reparations."
44 Ellen G. White, *Letter 36, 1880*, par. 4.

A Forgotten History of How Our Government Segregated America, details this form of discrimination. He argues that it won't be until Americans understand an accurate history of our nation's racial conflicts and division that we will be able to figure out a way to fulfill our legal and moral responsibilities.

While slavery and certain forms of discrimination may now be illegal in America, overt state-sanctioned racial violence, terrorism, and discrimination are much more recent than many realize. For example, Elizabeth Eckford was the first Black student to integrate into a white Southern high school – the Little Rock Central High School in Little Rock, Arkansas.[45] Eckford was born in 1941. Years later, she described the day she attempted to go, all alone, to a segregated school as a fifteen-year-old Black girl:

> I stood looking at the school – it looked so big! Just then the guards let some white students through. The crowd was quiet. I guess they were waiting to see what was going to happen. When I was able to steady my knees, I walked up to the guard who had let the white students in. He didn't move. When I tried to squeeze past him, he raised his bayonet, and then the other guards moved in and they raised their bayonets. They glared at me with a mean look and I was very frightened and didn't know what to do. I turned around and the crowd came toward me. They moved closer and closer. Somebody started yelling, "Lynch her! Lynch her!"[46]

Both victims and perpetrators of government-endorsed racial segregation and violent intimidation are still living today. Recent political events have merely torn the scab off of festering resentments among ethnic minorities fueled by widespread poverty,

---

45 David Margolick, *Elizabeth and Hazel: Two Women of Little Rock* (New Haven: Yale University Press, 2011), pp. 34–37, 47–51, 59–61, 80–82.
46 Steven Kasher, *The Civil Rights Movement: A Photographic History*, 1954–68 (New York: Abbeville Press, 1996), p. 54.

disproportionately high rates of incarceration, and harsher prison sentences.

Meanwhile, it wasn't just African Americans who were experiencing brutality and discrimination in the land of liberty. Early in our nation's history, Native Americans were slaughtered like animals. Their lands were stolen and treaties broken, even though, more recently, some official efforts toward reparations have been made (the Indian Claims Commission after the Second World War is one example). Asians and non-Anglo immigrants were treated as inferior. In the infamous case *Korematsu v. United States* (1944), the Supreme Court upheld the constitutionality of a presidential order that required American citizens of Japanese ancestry to be rounded up into internment camps. This for no other reason than that their appearance differed from the majority white population – and because they *might possibly* pose a national security threat.

Once again, keep in mind that many of these events aren't ancient history. Some of them happened during the lifetime of Americans still alive today – incidents that are etched into the memory of both victim and perpetrator. Far from being a thing of the distant past, state-sanctioned segregation, racial discrimination, and racial violence are relatively recent American history.

WHAT'S CHANGED?

But while laws serve to enforce someone's rights, they can't change the perpetrator's heart. And while laws have been enacted with the intent of eliminating many (though unfortunately not all) forms of racial discrimination, evil still lurks in the human heart. Only God's powerful love – manifested through us – can change the heart and bring about repentance, reconciliation, and forgiveness. We need the laws, but we also need God's love to make a lasting change.

Today, statistics show that people of color still experience racial discrimination – intentional or otherwise – in America's criminal justice system and beyond. In a system where only the wealthy can afford to post bail, pay court imposed fines, or hire effective legal counsel, people of color are disproportionately disadvantaged. According to the U.S. Department of Justice statistics as of 2014, approximately 12–13 percent of the American population is Black, but they make up 35 percent of jail inmates and 37 percent of prison inmates of the 2.2 million male inmates in American jails and prisons. EJI founder and public interest lawyer Bryan Stevenson has highlighted this issue in his captivating book *Just Mercy: A Story of Justice and Redemption*. Meanwhile, human rights groups point to a rise in xenophobia and overt racism in America. White supremacist hate groups, once thought to be dying out, have been emboldened by the recent political winds blowing across the land and are now becoming mainstream.

And of course there are the modern-day lynchings of people like Ahmaud Arbery, in which his murderer called him "F – ing N – " after he shot him three times with his shotgun, or the police brutality targeting African Americans, or the origins of police departments in the American South as slave patrols, or the fact that at least one researcher found that "the probability of being black, unarmed and shot by police is about 3.5 times the probability of being white, unarmed and shot by police," or the fact that Blacks are "more likely" than whites "to experience other types of force, including being handcuffed without arrest, pepper-sprayed or pushed to the ground by an officer."[47]

Disproportionate punishment based on race is nothing new. In 1899, White wrote:

The desire to show their masterly authority over the blacks is still burning in the hearts of many who claim to be Christians, but whose lives declare that they are standing under the black

---

47 https://plsonline.eku.edu/insidelook/history-policing-united-states-part-1 ; https://www.apa.org/monitor/2016/12/cover-policing.

banner of the great apostate. *When the whites commit crimes, they are often allowed to go uncondemned, while for the same transgressions the blacks...are treated worse than the brutes.* The demon of passion is let loose, and all the suffering that can be devised is instituted against them. Will not God judge for these things? As surely as the whites have brought their inhuman cruelty to bear upon the negroes, so surely will God's vengeance fall upon them.[48]

WHAT DO WE DO NOW?

You're probably thinking, "Most of this stuff happened in the past and it's not my fault!" However, the Bible teaches that we have a collective responsibility to do our best to make things right – even for the societal wrongs that may not be our fault. Daniel confessed the "sins of his people," even when there is no record that he participated in those sins. (See Daniel 9.) David made restitution to the Gibeonites for the actions of King Saul, even though he had nothing to do with Saul's actions. Once David made things right, the famine in the land, from which all Israel suffered, ceased. (See 2 Samuel 21.) As we've already seen, White understood this principle, arguing, thirty years after the Civil War, "The American nation owes a debt of love to the colored race, and God has ordained that they should make restitution for the wrong they have done them in the past." She then noted, *"Those who have taken no active part in enforcing slavery upon the colored people are not relieved from the responsibility of making special efforts to remove, as far as possible, the sure result of their enslavement."*[49]

White was simply echoing the Bible itself, where God commanded for restitution to be made to those who had been enslaved:

If any of your people – Hebrew men or women – sell themselves to you and serve you six years, in the seventh year you

---

48 Ellen G. White, *Letter 99, 1899*, par. 9, https://egwwritings.org.
49 Ellen G. White, "Am I My Brother's Keeper?" *The Review and Herald*, (January 21, 1896), par. 1.

must let them go free. And when you release them, *do not send them away empty-handed. Supply them liberally from your flock, your threshing floor and your winepress. Give to them as the Lord your God has blessed you.* Remember that you were slaves in Egypt and the Lord your God redeemed you. That is why I give you this command today (Deuteronomy 15: 12–15, NIV).

A few years earlier, in 1891, Ellen White had written to white Christians:

Are we not under even greater obligation to labor for the colored people than for those who have been more highly favored? *Who is it that held these people in servitude? Who kept them in ignorance, and pursued a course to debase and brutalize them, forcing them to disregard the law of marriage, breaking up the family relation, tearing wife from husband, and husband from wife?* If the race is degraded, if they are repulsive in habits and manners, who made them so? *Is there not much due to them from the white people?* After so great a wrong has been done them, should not an earnest effort be made to lift them up?[50]

Not much had changed by 1899, and again White called for restitution, writing:

The Lord demands restitution from the churches in America. You are to relieve the necessities of this field. In the day of final accounts men will not be pleased to meet the record of their deeds with reference to the books that have been prepared to help in carrying on the work in the South, by which means was diverted from the most needy portion of the Lord's vineyard.[51]

For most of our nation's history, the abominations of slavery, lynching, and racial terror were perpetuated in our land as an entire group of human beings was brutalized. Even today, the

---

50 Ellen G. White, *The Southern Work*, pp. 14–15.
51 Ibid., p. 95.

racism continues to manifest itself through both systems and individuals. Should we not be at least as honest and proactive as was King David in seeking to bring about justice, restitution, and reconciliation?

Many will argue that it is impossible to, in the words of White, "make restitution" to the Black race. Coates accurately observes that the

> idea of reparations is frightening not simply because we might lack the ability to pay. The idea of reparations threatens something much deeper – America's heritage, history, and standing in the world…[But] [t]o celebrate freedom and democracy while forgetting America's origins in a slavery economy is patriotism à la carte.[52]

Nevertheless, Christians should lead the way in this difficult discussion, for true racial reconciliation will never take place in America until we are willing to admit the truth and act upon it.

Of course, the greatest act of truth and reconciliation is the sacrifice of Jesus Christ on the cross. There, a truly innocent God demonstrated self-sacrificing love to solve a problem that was not His fault. "Beloved," John wrote, "if God so loved us, we also ought to love one another" (1 John 4:11, ESV). Nowhere is this kind of love more needed than in the divided world and church of today. God wants to heal the wounds caused by racism and bring every nation, tribe, tongue, and people together into one family.

TRUTH BEFORE RECONCILIATION

As Bryan Stevenson says, we can't have reconciliation unless we first know the truth. We need to talk about the truth of what has happened in the distant and more recent past, which still affects many alive today, and the systemic problems still in place today.

---

52 Coates, "The Case for Reparations."

Jesus is the ultimate answer to racism, and we need to focus more on Him than on the problems. But unfortunately, most American Christians don't even realize that racism is a problem. And *God can't save us from a sin we won't confess.* Focusing on Jesus, we ask, "What would Jesus do in this situation?" Jesus came "to set the oppressed free" (Luke 4:18), and He even rebuked the oppressors of His day. (See Matthew 23; Luke 19:45–48, etc.) While Christians are never called to condemn *people*, we are sometimes called to rebuke sin, and we are always called to "speak up for those who cannot speak for themselves, for the rights of all who are destitute" (Proverbs 31:8, NIV). The prophet Isaiah began his sermon on social justice with a call to

> Cry aloud; do not hold back; lift up your voice like a trumpet; declare to my people their transgression, to the house of Jacob their sins…Is not this the fast that I choose: to loose the bonds of wickedness, to undo the straps of the yoke, to let the oppressed go free, and to break every yoke? (Isaiah 58:1, 6, ESV).

Ellen White tied Isaiah's call for social justice to the issue of racism, writing about the hypocrisy of the "Christian" politicians of her day who would proclaim national days for fasting and prayer, and who,

> professing to have human hearts, have seen the slaves almost naked and starving, and have abused them, and sent them back to their cruel masters and hopeless bondage, to suffer inhuman cruelty for daring to seek their liberty. Some of this wretched class they thrust into unwholesome dungeons, to live or die, they cared not which. They have deprived them of the liberty and free air, which heaven has never denied them, and then left them to suffer for food and clothing. In view of all this, a national fast is proclaimed! Oh, what an insult to Jehovah! The Lord saith by the mouth of Isaiah: "Yet they seek Me daily,

and delight to know My ways, as a nation that did righteousness, and forsook not the ordinance of their God."[53]

So, what should we do now? Here's a place to start:

1. White American Christians need to lead the way by publicly confessing our complicity in the sins of white supremacy, slavery, racial violence, and institutionalized racism. We need to admit that we have participated in the sins of our ancestors through our attitudes and indifference, and that we have likely benefitted economically, educationally, socially, and otherwise at the expense of people of color. Only when we admit there is a problem can healing begin.

2. We need to recognize that we – the American nation and people – have never made restitution to the enslaved or their descendants, even as much of our prosperity and wealth as a nation have been the result of the slave labor of Black Americans. Baptist, in his book *The Half Has Never Been Told: Slavery and the Making of American Capitalism,* uncovers the history of how America's prosperity was built largely on the backs of enslaved Blacks and how we as a nation have yet to pay back that debt we owe them. We need to genuinely consider how to make restitution for the generational wrongs done to Blacks in America.

3. Finally, Ellen White said it best: "Walls of separation have been built up between the whites and the blacks. These walls of prejudice will tumble down of themselves as did the walls of Jericho, when Christians obey the word of God, which enjoins on them supreme love to their maker and impartial love to their neighbors. *For Christ's sake, let us do something now.*"[54]

---

53 Ellen G. White, *Testimonies for the Church,* vol. 1, p. 257.
54 Ellen G. White, "An Example in History," *The Review and Herald,* (Dec. 17, 1895), par. 5.

The early Christian church shows us how to deal with the issue of racism. In Acts chapter 6, we find that "the Hellenistic Jews among them complained against the Hebraic Jews because their widows were being overlooked in the daily distribution of food" (Acts 6:1, NIV). Instead of ignoring the allegations and hoping they'd go away, the church leaders did the right thing. "Brothers and sisters, choose seven men from among you who are known to be full of the Spirit and wisdom. We will turn this responsibility over to them" (Acts 6:3, NIV). The voice of those alleging unfairness was heard, and, interestingly, those chosen to deal with the problem were apparently all from among the Hellenistic Jews. "This proposal pleased the whole group," and as a result, "the word of God spread. The number of disciples in Jerusalem increased rapidly" (Acts 6:5, 7, NIV).

TAKE ACTION: DO JUSTICE NOW

- How can I lead the way by confronting racism in my own heart?

- One way I will commit to reaching out and helping the Black community is:

- One civil rights organization that I will support financially or otherwise is:

"And he lifted up his eyes on
his disciples, and said, Blessed be ye poor:
for yours is the kingdom of God....
But woe unto you that are rich!
for ye have received your consolation"
LUKE 6:20, 24, KJV

"Is not this the fast
that I have chosen? to loose the bands
of wickedness, to undo the heavy burdens,
and to let the oppressed go free,
and that ye break every yoke?"
ISAIAH 58:6, KJV.

CHAPTER FOUR
ECONOMIC JUSTICE

I'll never forget Ruben.[55] I was a youth pastor at a large city church when I met him. He was in his early twenties but had the mentality of a young child. His disheveled appearance, strong body odor, and strange speech patterns made it clear that Ruben was different. Because of his developmental and mental disabilities, Ruben received a small government check each month. For the first part of the month, Ruben would usually live in a cheap motel until his funds ran out, and then he would set up his tent somewhere to live outdoors until his next check came.

Ruben was just one of many people with physical or mental limitations whose lives intersected with the church where I worked. Even though our church sponsored a weekly food giveaway and participated in a winter program to shelter homeless people, the needs of the poor far exceeded what the church alone could provide. Even with all the area churches working together, something more was needed. As a pastor, I was thankful for the role that government played in helping Ruben and others like him.

Most will agree that someone like Ruben needs help to make it in the world. But other situations are less clear. What about the guy who isn't disabled but is just down on his luck? Or the lady whose own poor choices have contributed to health problems, making it impossible for her to work?

---

55 Not his real name.

SHOULD GOVERNMENT HELP THE POOR?

When it comes to helping the poor and disabled, it seems like Christians fall into one of two camps: those who believe that help to the poor should only come from voluntary charity and those who believe that government has a legitimate role to play in helping the poor.

It's beyond the scope of this chapter to examine in detail what it means to really *help* the poor. The main focus here is to answer two questions: first, how should Christians relate to wealth and poverty? Second, is there a legitimate role for government to play in helping the poor?

WEALTH AND POVERTY IN THE BIBLE

First, the Bible discourages the pursuit of extreme wealth and warns against the dangers of being rich: "Give me neither poverty nor riches, but give me only my daily bread. Otherwise, I may have too much and disown you and say, 'Who is the Lord?' Or I may become poor and steal, and so dishonor the name of my God" (Proverbs 30:8–9, NIV).

> But godliness with contentment is great gain. For we brought nothing into the world, and we can take nothing out of it. But if we have food and clothing, we will be content with that. *Those who want to get rich fall into temptation and a trap* and into many foolish and harmful desires that plunge people into ruin and destruction. *For the love of money is a root of all kinds of evil.* Some people, *eager for money*, have wandered from the faith and pierced themselves with many griefs (1 Timothy 6:6–10, NIV).

The dominant theology of Jesus' day was essentially a prosperity gospel. Those who were successful were considered blessed of God; the poor and sick were viewed as less favored of God – or even cursed. In this context, Jesus startled His disciples by proclaiming: "How hard it is for the rich to enter the kingdom of

God!…It is easier for a camel to go through the eye of a needle than for someone who is rich to enter the kingdom of God" (Mark 10:23, 25, NIV).

God had reminded the Israelites that their own skill alone was not responsible for their financial success: "You may say to yourself, 'My power and the strength of my hands have produced this wealth for me.' But remember the Lord your God, for it is he who gives you the ability to produce wealth" (Deuteronomy 8:17–18, NIV).

The Bible recognizes that some people are just better at money than others. For example, God told the Israelites that there "will always be poor people in the land. Therefore I command you [the rich] to be openhanded toward your fellow Israelites who are poor and needy in your land" (Deuteronomy 15:11, NIV). (However, see also Deuteronomy 15:4–5, NRSV, where God declared that if Israel were to follow His laws with regard to poverty there would "be no one in need among you." More on that in a moment.)

The Bible tells us that some people are poor through no fault of their own and that we are to give them aid: "If any of your fellow Israelites become poor and are unable to support themselves among you, help them as you would a foreigner and stranger, so they can continue to live among you" (Leviticus 25:35, NIV). And still others are poor because of their own laziness: "How long will you lie there, you sluggard? When will you get up from your sleep?…Poverty will come on you like a thief and scarcity like an armed man" (Proverbs 6:9,11 NIV).

Paul taught that Christians should not be unproductive or poor because of their own idleness, writing, "Our people must learn to devote themselves to doing what is good, in order to provide for urgent needs and not live unproductive lives" (Titus 3:14, NIV).

You should mind your own business and work with your hands, just as we told you, so that your daily life may win the respect of outsiders and so that you will not be dependent on anybody…For even when we were with you, we gave you this rule: "The one who is unwilling to work shall not eat" (1 Thessalonians 4:11–12; 2 Thessalonians 3:10, NIV).

However, as Timothy Keller notes, it's important to remember:

The Bible does not teach that your success or failure is wholly due to individual choices. Poverty for example, can be brought on by personal failure (Proverbs 6:6–7; 23:21), but it may also exist because of environmental factors such as famine or plague, or sheer injustice (Proverbs 13:23; cf. Exodus 22:21–27). So we are not in complete control of our life outcomes.[56]

The Bible recognizes the human tendency to favor those who are rich and successful. (See, e.g., James 2:1–9.) James, however, reminded his listeners that it was the rich who were "exploiting" them. "Are they not the ones who are dragging you into court?" (James 2:6, NIV). He urged his listeners to guard against prejudice toward the poor, writing that "if you show favoritism, you sin" (James 2:9, NIV). The Bible also makes it clear that we are not to show partiality to the poor (Leviticus 19:15). But the Bible also tells us that those who "consider the poor" are blessed and that "the Lord will deliver him in time of trouble," and it commands us to "plead the cause of the poor and needy" (Psalm 41:1; Proverbs 31:9, NKJV). White notes that "[t]here is a link that connects Christ with the poor in a special sense."[57] And Keller aptly observes,

This is not a contradiction…The Bible doesn't say "speak up for the rich and powerful," not because they are less important as persons before God, but because they don't need you to do this. The playing field is not level and if we don't advocate for

---

56 Keller, *A Biblical Critique of Secular Justice and Critical Theory.*

57 Ellen G. White, *The Southern Work*, p. 85.

the poor there will not be equality. In this aspect of justice, we are seeking to give more social, financial, and cultural capital (power) to those with less. Jeremiah 22:3 says "Protect the person who is being cheated from the one who is mistreating... foreigners, orphans, or widows...." Jeremiah is singling out for protection groups of people who can't protect themselves from mistreatment the way others can. (cf. Zechariah 7:9–10).[58]

Jesus, Himself a poor man during His life on earth, defended the poor. While His ministry consisted almost entirely of healing, teaching, and preaching, one event of "social activism" stands out for the passion that Jesus showed in defending both the sacredness of His Father's house and the cause of the poor:

Jesus entered the temple courts and drove out all who were buying and selling there. He overturned the tables of the money changers and the benches of those selling doves. "It is written," he said to them, "'My house will be called a house of prayer,' but you are making it 'a den of robbers.'" (Matthew 21:12–13, NIV).

The story of the cleansing of the temple (which happened twice; see John 2:11–12) illustrates God's concern for social justice and the cause of the poor. The house of worship had been coopted by greedy businessmen intent on exploiting the helpless worshippers who came seeking a sacrificial animal and the temple currency to pay the annual tax. In commanding these thieves to vacate the temple, Jesus manifested "a zeal and severity" never before seen.[59] And for what purpose? To defend the poor and needy from exploitation and the house of God from this iniquitous racket.

---

58 Keller, *A Biblical Critique of Secular Justice and Critical Theory.*
59 Ellen G. White, *The Desire of Ages,* p. 158.

OLD TESTAMENT LAW AND THE NEW COVENANT

Some have wondered whether God's admonitions and laws regarding the poor are still applicable to followers of Jesus living under the New Covenant. The New Covenant is God's promise to write His laws of love in our hearts so that we will obey them. Jesus said that all the Law and the Prophets "hang" on the two great commandments of supreme love for God and loving our neighbor as ourselves. The Ten Commandments, written in stone by the finger of God, are the natural outgrowth of the two great commands. And this is the same law that God promises to write on our hearts (Hebrews 8:10). Even though the New Covenant experience is available to everyone, not everyone will consent to God writing His law in their heart. While God will never force anyone to *worship* Him (and neither will His followers), the Bible tells us that we still need civil laws that regulate certain *behavior* and prevent people from harming each other (see, e.g., Romans 13). Many of the civil laws that God gave to the Israelites contain principles that can be applicable to society today – chief among them are the civil laws concerning economic justice for the poor.

WHAT ROLE SHOULD GOVERNMENT PLAY IN HELPING THE POOR?

While the Bible's overall focus is on the spiritual kingdom of God, it isn't completely silent about politics or the role of earthly government. The Apostle Paul addressed the issue most explicitly in his epistle to the Romans, where he states that God has put political rulers in place to punish those who "do what is wrong" (Romans 13:4).[60]

---

60 It's unfortunate, but not surprising, that corrupt politicians have appropriated Paul's message in Romans 13 to justify their oppressive regimes. But Paul's command to "be subject to the governing authorities" must be understood within the wider context of Scripture. In short, Romans 13 doesn't

While the church is called to advance the *spiritual* kingdom of God on earth (as opposed to setting up a *political* version of the kingdom of God), followers of Jesus should advocate for the governments of which they are citizens to be moral, just, and good.

Does the Bible give us any idea of what a moral, just, and good government looks like? It does. Ancient Israel was a theocracy – God's kingdom on earth – and many of its civil laws provide examples of what a moral and just society can look like. While we cannot and should not draw a straight line between the civil laws of a theocracy and the laws a secular government should enact, we can gather some general principles. While many of the Mosaic laws, such as the laws regarding sacrifices and annual feast days, were spiritual laws that were "shadows" pointing forward to the coming Messiah, some of the Mosaic civil laws were not inherently spiritual or related to worship. *In other words, some of the Mosaic civil laws are clearly inapplicable outside a theocracy, but others may provide principles that can inspire civil governments today.*

Early Adventists saw certain Mosaic civil laws as applying to the modern world.[61] For example, they understood the command of Deuteronomy 23:15 – "You shall not give back to his master the slave who has escaped from his master to you" (NKJV) – as applicable to nineteenth-century Americans. Ellen G. White wrote, "Where the laws of men conflict with God's word and law, we are to obey the word and law of God, whatever the consequences may be. *The laws of our land requiring us to deliver a slave to his master, we are not to obey,* and we must abide the consequences of the violation of this law. This slave is not the property of any man. God is his rightful Master, and man has no right to take God's workmanship into his hands, and claim his as his own."[62]

---

require Christians to blindly obey governments if doing so would cause them to disobey God. See, for example, Acts 5:29.

61 For a discussion on which biblical principles are applicable to modern secular governments, see Chapter 5.

62 Ellen G. White, *Spiritual Gifts,* vol. 4b, pp. 42–43, https://egwwritings.org.

In Chapter 1, we saw that God gave the Israelites civil laws regarding the treatment of the poor:

- The law of the land required all debts to be forgiven every seven years. "At the end of every seven years you must cancel debts" (Deuteronomy 15:1, NIV).

- Every fifty years, the law required that land reverted to the original owners. "In this Year of Jubilee everyone is to return to their own property" (Leviticus 25:13, NIV).

- Numerous other biblical passages condemn the oppression of workers and command employers to pay a fair wage to their employees. "Do not hold back the wages of a hired worker overnight" (Leviticus 19:13, NIV). "So I will come to put you on trial. I will be quick to testify...against those who defraud laborers of their wages...but do not fear me," says the Lord Almighty (Malachi 3:5, NIV). "Now listen, you rich people, weep and wail because of the misery that is coming on you... Look! The wages you failed to pay the workers who mowed your fields are crying out against you" (James 5:1, 4, NIV).

Knowing that God gave Israel civil laws that benefitted the poor, should governments enact similar types of laws today? As requiring taxes is a legitimate role of government (see, e.g., Romans 13:7), what if a government uses some of that revenue to aid the poor? As we will see, White seemed to think that secular civil government had a role in helping the less fortunate and promoting "social equality." God's civil laws for ancient Israel show us that relying on the generosity of the selfish human heart is not enough; legal structures and regulations are needed to help promote equality of opportunity.

In fact, the Bible teaches that a government that ignores poverty – or worse yet, encourages oppression of the poor – is an *immoral* government:

Woe to those who decree iniquitous decrees, and the writers who keep writing oppression, to turn aside the needy from justice and to rob the poor of my people of their right, that widows may be their spoil, and that they may make the fatherless their prey! What will you do on the day of punishment, in the ruin that will come from afar? To whom will you flee for help, and where will you leave your wealth? (Isaiah 10:1–3, ESV).

WHAT WAS THE ULTIMATE GOAL OF GOD'S LAWS FOR THE POOR?

Some have used the words of Jesus – "The poor you will always have with you, but you will not always have me" (Matthew 26:11, NIV) – to justify doing nothing about poverty. As the poor will "always" be with us, should we throw up our hands in resignation? On closer examination, we find that Jesus was simply stating the reality of life in this sinful world. The words of Jesus were taken from Deuteronomy 15:11. Notice that the full passage actually includes a command about how to treat the poor: "There will always be poor people in the land. *Therefore I command you to be openhanded toward your fellow Israelites who are poor and needy in your land*" (NIV). Poverty is not God's ideal. In fact, when Jesus Himself inspired Moses to write Deuteronomy, only a few verses prior, Moses wrote God's ultimate goal with regard to poverty: "There will, however, *be no one in need among you*, because the Lord is sure to bless you in the land that the Lord your God is giving you as a possession to occupy, if only you will obey the Lord your God by diligently observing this entire commandment that I command you today" (Deuteronomy 15:4–5, NRSV). In other words, if the economic laws God gave Israel were put into practice, poverty would ultimately cease to be a problem.

BABYLON - A GOVERNMENT
THAT OPPRESSED THE POOR

The kingdom of Babylon presents a case study in government gone bad – a government that oppressed the poor. In Daniel chapter 4, God warned King Nebuchadnezzar in a dream that if he failed to acknowledge the true source of his power, he would be humbled. The Government of Babylon was illustrated by a great tree:

> The tree grew large and strong and its top touched the sky; it was visible to the ends of the earth. Its leaves were beautiful, its fruit abundant, and on it was food for all. Under it the wild animals found shelter, and the birds lived in its branches; from it every creature was fed (Daniel 4:11–12, NIV).

"This representation shows the character of a government that fulfills God's purpose – a government that protects and upbuilds the nation."[63] However:

> Instead of being a protector of men, Babylon became a proud and cruel oppressor. The words of Inspiration picturing the cruelty and greed of rulers in Israel reveal the secret of Babylon's fall and of the fall of many another kingdom since the world began: "Ye eat the fat, and ye clothe you with the wool, ye kill them that are fed: but ye feed not the flock. The diseased have ye not strengthened, neither have ye healed that which was sick, neither have ye bound up that which was broken, neither have ye brought again that which was driven away, neither have ye sought that which was lost; but with force and with cruelty have ye ruled them" (Ezekiel 34:3, 4).[64]

The prophet Daniel warned the king with the following words: "Your Majesty, be pleased to accept my advice: Renounce your

---

63 Ellen G. White, *Education*, p. 175, https://egwwritings.org.
64 Ibid., p. 176.

sins by doing what is right, and your wickedness *by being kind to the oppressed*. It may be that then your prosperity will continue" (Daniel 4:27, NIV). White commented, noting that

> In the dream of Nebuchadnezzar *the true object of government is beautifully represented by the great tree* "whose leaves were fair, and the fruit thereof much, and in it was meat for all; under which the beasts of the field dwelt, and upon whose branches the fowls of the heaven had their habitation."…That representation of the tree shows the only kind of ruling acceptable to Him – *a government that protects, restores, relieves, but never savors of oppression. The poor especially are to be kindly treated.*[65]

The Government of Babylon fulfilled God's purposes when it protected the poor, provided for the sick, and was kind to the oppressed. God's purpose for secular governments today is no different.

ELLEN WHITE'S VIEW: NOT COMMUNISM OR UNBRIDLED CAPITALISM

After the American Civil War, White believed that the United States Government had a crucial role to play in caring for and educating those who had been formerly enslaved:

> Much might have been accomplished by the people of America if adequate efforts in behalf of the freedmen had been put forth by the Government and by the Christian churches immediately after the emancipation of the slaves. Money should have been used freely to care for and educate them at the time they were so greatly in need of help. But the Government, after a little effort, left the Negro to struggle, unaided, with his burden of difficulties. Some of the strong Christian churches began a good work, but sadly failed to reach more than a comparatively few; and the Seventh-day

---

65 Ellen G. White, *Manuscript 29, 1895*, par. 18, https://egwwritings.org.

Adventist Church has failed to act its part. Some persevering efforts have been put forth by individuals and by societies to uplift the colored people, and a noble work has been done. But how few have had a part in this work which should have had the sympathy and help of all![66]

In White's view, secular government had a role to play in helping the freed slaves. It wasn't just the church's job to help the impoverished formerly enslaved; the government was to help as well.

White wrote that the Mosaic economic "regulations" promoted "social order" and "the stability of government" and saw human beings as interconnected on a socio-economic level:

There is nothing, after their recognition of the claims of God, that more distinguishes the laws given by Moses than the liberal, tender, and hospitable spirit enjoined toward the poor… These regulations were designed to bless the rich no less than the poor. They would restrain avarice and a disposition for self-exaltation, and would cultivate a noble spirit of benevolence; and by fostering good will and confidence between all classes, *they would promote social order, the stability of government. We are all woven together in the great web of humanity, and whatever we can do to benefit and uplift others will reflect in blessing upon ourselves.*[67]

White believed that "[t]here is no sin in being rich if riches are not acquired by injustice. A rich man is not condemned for having riches, but condemnation rests upon him if the means entrusted to him is spent in selfishness."[68] She also did not believe that communism, as an economic system, was the answer, writing:

There are many who urge with great enthusiasm that all men should have an equal share in the temporal blessings of God.

---

66 Ellen G. White, *Testimonies for the Church*, vol. 9, p. 205, https://egwwritings.org.

67 Ellen G. White, *Patriarchs and Prophets*, pp. 530, 534–535.

68 Ellen G. White, *Christ's Object Lessons*, p. 266, https://egwwritings.org.

But this was not the purpose of the Creator. A diversity of condition is one of the means by which God designs to prove and develop character. Yet He intends that those who have worldly possessions shall regard themselves merely as stewards of His goods, as entrusted with means to be employed for the benefit of the suffering and the needy.[69]

However, White did not believe in unfettered capitalism either. White believed that government had a role to play in regulating the "continued accumulation of wealth" and in promoting "social equality." She also believed that God, in His wisdom, had placed legal checks and balances in place in the government of Israel to temper the effects of human greed.

The Lord would place a check upon the inordinate love of property and power. Great evils would result from the continued accumulation of wealth by one class, and the poverty and degradation of another...There would be a feeling of despair and desperation which would tend to demoralize society and open the door to crimes of every description. *The regulations that God established were designed to promote social equality.* The provisions of the sabbatical year and the jubilee would, in a great measure, set right that which during the interval had gone wrong in the social and political economy of the nation.[70]

White also believed that the economic laws given by God could have continued, and that much of today's societal unrest can be traced to selfishness and economic inequality:

If the law given by God for the benefit of the poor had continued to be carried out, how different would be the present condition of the world, morally, spiritually, and temporally! Selfishness and self-importance would not be manifested as now, but each

---

69 Ibid., p. 535.
70 Ibid., p. 534.

would cherish a kind regard for the happiness and welfare of others; and such widespread destitution as is now seen in many lands would not exist. *The principles which God has enjoined, would prevent the terrible evils that in all ages have resulted from the oppression of the rich toward the poor and the suspicion and hatred of the poor toward the rich.* While they might hinder the amassing of great wealth and the indulgence of unbounded luxury, they would prevent the consequent ignorance and degradation of tens of thousands whose ill-paid servitude is required to build up these colossal fortunes. *They would bring a peaceful solution of those problems that now threaten to fill the world with anarchy and bloodshed.*[71]

During the free silver economic policy debate of the late nineteenth century, White discouraged ministers from "taking sides in regard to these questions that the Lord did not lay upon them the burden to engage in," and later wrote that when God's "voice is obeyed, ye will not give your voice or influence to any policy to enrich a few, to bring oppression and suffering to the poorer class of humanity."[72] Yet, White spoke out against economic injustice and spared no words for those who, in her words, hoarded wealth:

How long will the Lord suffer oppression of the poor that rich men may hoard wealth? These men are heaping together treasures for the last days. Their money is placed where it does no one any good. To add to their millions, they rob the poor, and the cries of the starving are no more to them than the barking of a dog. But the Lord marks every act of oppression. No cry of suffering is unheard by Him. Those who today are scheming to obtain more and more money, putting in operation plans that mean to the poor starvation, will in the last great day stand face to face with their deeds of oppression and injustice.[73]

---

71 Ibid., p. 536.
72 Ellen G. White, *Testimonies to Ministers,* p. 332, https://egwwritings.org..
73 Ellen G. White, *Letter 201, 1902,* par. 10, https://egwwritings.org.

GOD'S IDEAL FOR THE CHURCH

While our world will never fully reflect God's ideal, Jesus Himself has shown His followers the way. For Christians, following Jesus means more than merely advocating for economic justice on a societal level. While it is perfectly appropriate for a secular government to tax its citizens in order to appropriately assist the poor, God's goal is for His people to also have a heart for the poor. In the words of the Apostle John: "If anyone has material possessions and sees a brother or sister in need but has no pity on them, how can the love of God be in that person? Dear children, let us not love with words or speech but with actions and in truth" (1 John 3:17–18, NIV).

The Bible starts with the foundational principle that we are not our own – we have been bought with a price (1 Corinthians 6:20). The infinite sacrifice of Jesus Christ was the price paid for our redemption, and it is because Jesus gave up everything for us that we recognize all we have and are as His. "For you know the grace of our Lord Jesus Christ, that though he was rich, yet for your sake he became poor, so that you through his poverty might become rich" (2 Corinthians 8:9, NIV).

God has a claim on all of our assets because "it is he who gives you the ability to produce wealth" (Deuteronomy 8:17–18, NIV). As a reminder of this, He asks us to return to Him 10 percent of our increase (a tithe) and offerings as well:

But you ask, "How are we robbing you?" "In tithes and offerings. You are under a curse – your whole nation – because you are robbing me. Bring the whole tithe into the storehouse, that there may be food in my house. Test me in this," says the Lord Almighty, "and see if I will not throw open the floodgates of heaven and pour out so much blessing that there will not be room enough to store it" (Malachi 3:8–10, NIV).

The "offerings" Malachi refers to harken back to the second tithe that the Israelites were commanded to give (Deuteronomy

14:23, 29; 26:12). This tithe was to be used both for a thank offering and for a religious feast "in which the Levite, the stranger, the fatherless, and the widow should participate." Also, "this tithe would provide a fund for the uses of charity and hospitality."[74] Finally, God's command to the Israelites was straightforward: "If anyone is poor among your fellow Israelites in any of the towns of the land the Lord your God is giving you, do not be hardhearted or tightfisted toward them. Rather, be openhanded and freely lend them whatever they need" (Deuteronomy 15:7–8, NIV). In New Testament times, the Apostle Paul wrote along similar lines to the prosperous church at Corinth regarding the impoverished Macedonian believers: "It is a question of a fair balance between your present abundance and their need…As it is written, 'The one who had much did not have too much, and the one who had little did not have too little'" (2 Corinthians 8:13–15, NRSV).

The principles of unselfish love will be written into the hearts of those who claim the New Covenant promise. Nevertheless, we need wisdom to know how to really help the poor. Sometimes, giving money is the best solution to someone's problems, but other times, we need to journey with someone, find out about their life, and help them find the tools to deal with the root of the problem. "If any of you lacks wisdom, you should ask God, who gives generously to all" (James 1:5, NIV). Whatever God calls us to do, we must remember that we are merely stewards of all that God has given us – to be used for His glory to help those in need. For those who, like Jesus, live to bless others, there's a promise: "Good will come to those who are generous and lend freely, who conduct their affairs with justice" (Psalm 112:5, NIV).

---

74 Ellen G. White, *Patriarchs and Prophets*, p. 530.

THE WAY OF THE KINGDOM

Paul tells us that "the love of money is a root of all kinds of evil" (1 Timothy 6:10, NIV), and the biblical portrait of false religion certainly bears this out. In Revelation 18, John the Revelator describes the fall of Babylon. Babylon, a symbol of false religion in the Bible, is described as a prostitute living in luxury and wealth that was built by oppression and extortion. "Woe! Woe to you, great city, dressed in fine linen, purple and scarlet, and glittering with gold, precious stones and pearls! In one hour such great wealth has been brought to ruin!" (Revelation 18:16–17, NIV). Yet the Kingdom of God subverts all that Babylon represents. The gold, precious stones, and pearls that Babylon worships become the pavement and common building materials in the New Jerusalem, and the citizens of that coming kingdom, instead of loving money, have chosen Jesus as their Master (Matthew 6:24).

Jesus, in announcing His kingdom mission, proclaimed, "The Spirit of the Lord is upon me, because he has anointed me to proclaim good news to the poor...to proclaim the year of the Lord's favor" (Luke 4:18–19, ESV). Jesus' listeners in the Nazareth synagogue that day thought of the year of Jubilee – the day of the Lord's favor – when the reset button was to be pushed, debts were to be forgiven, slaves were to be set free, and the land was to be returned to the original owner. Jubilee was a foretaste of the kingdom of heaven on earth!

After thirty-three years of living a life of other-centered love, Jesus laid down His life in a supreme act of unselfishness, was resurrected three days later, and went back to heaven. He sent the Holy Spirit to a little band of believers in an upper room. Israel hadn't fulfilled its destiny to showcase heaven on earth, but would the new band of believers live as citizens of God's kingdom? Would love for their King compel them to live like that?

The answer was yes! It was that early group of Christians who modeled for the rest of the world what the kingdom of God can look like when God's people take seriously the words of Deuteronomy 15:4–5: "There will, however, *be no one in need among you*, because the Lord is sure to bless you…if only you will obey the Lord your God by diligently observing this entire commandment that I command you today" (NRSV). The story goes that "All the believers were together and had everything in common. They sold property and possessions to give to anyone who had need" (Acts 2:44–45, NIV). "God's grace was so powerfully at work in them all that *there were no needy persons among them*" (Acts 4:33–34, NIV). In contrast to the religionists of Isaiah's day, who were engaged in daily worship but exploiting their workers (see Isaiah 58:2–3), the early Christians understood that worship without social justice was hypocritical, and they put into practice the admonition of James that "religion that God our Father accepts as pure and faultless is this: to look after orphans and widows in their distress and to keep oneself from being polluted by the world" (James 1:27, NIV).

What happened in the book of Acts is an illustration of what God can do in and through His church. In a day and age when selfishness often seems to be a virtue, God wants His church to lead the way by example, praying for wisdom to know how to truly help those in need and then doing her part.

Does secular government also have a part to play in tackling the problem of poverty? Absolutely. In a world as complex as ours, philanthropy is not an adequate substitute for systems that alleviate poverty, and the church is not in a position to create or maintain those systems without making that work the sole focus of its mission.[75] The church should advocate for economic justice by encouraging the kind of government that shows "mercy to the poor" (Daniel 4:27, KJV), "a government that protects, restores, relieves, but never savors of oppression" where the "poor

---

75 White argued that "[t]he work of seeking the outcasts is important, but it is not to become the great burden of [the church's] mission." Ellen G. White, *Welfare Ministry*, p. 258, https://egwwritings.org.

especially are...kindly treated."[76] White's vision for economic justice was revolutionary. She believed that God's principles of economic justice, if put into practice, would radically alter the present condition of our world:

> If the law given by God for the benefit of the poor had con-
> tinued to be carried out, how different would be the present
> condition of the world, morally, spiritually, and temporally!...
> *The principles which God has enjoined, would prevent the terrible evils that*
> *in all ages have resulted from the oppression of the rich toward the poor*
> *and the suspicion and hatred of the poor toward the rich.* While they
> might hinder the amassing of great wealth and the indulgence
> of unbounded luxury, they would prevent the consequent
> ignorance and degradation of tens of thousands whose ill-paid
> servitude is required to build up these colossal fortunes.
> *They would bring a peaceful solution of those problems that now threaten*
> *to fill the world with anarchy and bloodshed.*[77]

76 Ellen G. White, *Manuscript 29*, 1895, par. 18.
77 Ellen G. White, *Patriarchs and Prophets*, p. 536.

TAKE ACTION: DO JUSTICE NOW

- How can I partner with my local church and community to help those in need?

- What are some ways I can truly help the needy while not enabling dysfunction?

- I commit to contacting (name of person) _____ within the next day and offering to help them in the following way(s):

"Speak up for those who cannot speak for themselves, for the rights of all who are destitute. Speak up and judge fairly; defend the rights of the poor and needy"

PROVERBS 31:8-9, NIV

CHAPTER FIVE

CHURCH, STATE, AND PUBLIC MORALITY

Today's evangelical Christian culture warriors proclaim that America is a Christian nation, by which they mean that America's Government should be a Christian one. Believing this to be true, many engage in the all-out war over gay marriage, abortion, the role of religion in public life, and a myriad of other issues. Their vision for a Christian nation does not usually include racial and economic justice, or other issues like caring for the earth.

Is this author advocating for a Christian nation – only of a different kind, with a focus on issues such as helping the poor and righting the wrongs caused by racism? No. In the two chapters that follow, we explore the intersection between social justice and separation of church and state. It's a nuanced discussion, with no easy answers, but one that we must engage in if we want to truly do justice in the world. In short, both social justice and separation of church and state are biblical goals we ought to pursue.

* * * * *

Imagine a group of people moving to an uninhabited island with the goal of establishing the ideal society. They decide to make the Ten Commandments the law of the land. This would, of course, include enforcing the first four commandments, which command us to worship God. Dissenters are punished for breaking any of the commandments.

To some, this may sound like a good idea. Why shouldn't Christians want to set up a government that enforces God's law and advances His kingdom? But recall what Jesus said about His kingdom being fundamentally different from worldly political systems, with completely different goals. "My kingdom is not from this world," He said. "If my kingdom were from this world, my followers would be fighting...But as it is, my kingdom is not from here" (John 18:36, NRSV). In other words, Christ's followers are not called to set up a *political* version of the kingdom of God on earth but instead to advance the *spiritual* kingdom of God. (See Appendix B for a discussion on why God no longer reigns on earth through a theocracy.)

Ellen G. White chimed in on this topic, writing:

> To protect liberty of conscience is the duty of the state, and this is the limit of its authority in matters of religion. Every secular government that attempts to regulate or enforce religious observances by civil authority is sacrificing the very principle for which the evangelical Christian so nobly struggled.[78]

In fact, White laid the blame for all "religious laws" and persecution squarely at the feet of a backslidden Christian church:

> Finding herself destitute of the power of love, [the church] has reached out for the strong arm of the state to enforce her dogmas and execute her decrees. Here is the secret of all religious laws that have ever been enacted, and the secret of all persecution from the days of Abel to our own time.[79]

As an alternative to a government where religion controls the state, consider Roger Williams, who created the "first government in the world which broke church and state apart."[80] Rhode Island was also revolutionary in other ways. "It outlawed slavery – an extraordinary action, likely the first in the world, and a reflection

---

78 Ellen G. White, *The Great Controversy*, p. 201, https://egwwritings.org.
79 Ellen G. White, *Thoughts from the Mount of Blessing*, p. 127.
80 John M. Barry, *Roger Williams and the Creation of the American Soul: Church, State, and the Birth of Liberty* (New York: Penguin Books, 2012), p. 389.

of the beliefs of...Williams."[81] Williams understood the principle of liberty of conscience, something he called "soul liberty," which led him to believe in separation of church and state. Williams, who had a deep, personal commitment to Jesus, noted that Christians should be the first to erect a wall of separation between the garden of the church and the wilderness of the world, or the state. "Forced worship," Williams said, "stinks in God's nostrils," and Williams compared coercive religious laws to "spiritual rape."[82] Williams "also believed that laws designed simply to create a moral society – as when Calvin outlawed playing cards, dice, or ninepins in Geneva – breached the wall between the garden of the church and the wilderness of the world."[83] Williams' radical ideas on separation of church and state led to yet another revolutionary concept – the idea that political authority did not necessarily come from God but rather "that the state derives its authority from and remains subject to its citizens."[84] As a result, "Rhode Island, became the asylum of the oppressed, and it increased and prospered until its foundation principles – civil and religious liberty – became the cornerstones of the American Republic."[85] Many of the ideas that Williams championed were later enshrined in our Constitution and Bill of Rights.

Yet, when James Madison, the father of the Constitution, wrote the First Amendment, "Congress shall make no law respecting an establishment of religion, or prohibiting the free exercise thereof," it was controversial, to say the least. The state-funded churches in the American colonies and many American pastors and politicians didn't like the idea that the church would no longer have supreme power over the state. Historians Isaac Kramnick and R. Laurence Moore detail an instance of resistance in which colonial religious leaders in Virginia sent

---

81 Ibid., p. 356.
82 Ibid., p. 336.
83 Ibid., p. 332.
84 Ibid., p. 389.
85 Ellen G. White, *The Great Controversy*, p. 295.

a letter to the delegates at the Virginia ratifying convention in June 1788, urging them to add a clause to the first or second article of the Constitution requiring the creation of "academies regulated by Congress where young people would learn 'the principles of the Christian religion without regard to any sect.'"[86] The founding fathers wisely rejected this and other similar ideas, probably because many of them had experienced firsthand the results of mixing church and state in England – and they knew the results weren't pretty!

> So successful were the drafters of the Constitution in defining government in secular terms that one of the most powerful criticisms of the Constitution when ratified and for succeeding decades was that it was indifferent to Christianity and God. It was denounced by many as a godless document, which is precisely what it was.[87]

The Bill of Rights was finally ratified, limiting the church's power by effectively erecting a metaphorical wall between the church and the state. Of the Founding Fathers, Kramnick and Moore write:

> Despite, or rather because of, [their] passionate concern for morality, the founding fathers made no constitutional provision for the national government to instruct its citizens in matters of moral and religious conscience. They did not want America to be godless, only its government. *How, then, did they imagine that a democratic state could ensure that its citizens would incorporate moral codes into private conscience? The simple answer is that they did not.* A democratic government was not created to produce moral citizens. It was the other way around: moral citizens constructed and preserved democracy. The founders left the business of

---

86 Isaac Kramnick and R. Laurence Moore, *The Godless Constitution: A Moral Defense of the Secular State* (New York: W.W. Norton & Company, 2005), p. 36.
87 Ibid., p. 23.

teaching morality to private concerns, a principle that should carry some weight with present-day conservatives.[88]

The new Constitution provided that "no religious test" would be required to hold public office in the new federal government. Many Christians of the day vigorously opposed this provision, as they feared it would open the door to Jews, Catholics, and Quakers serving in public office. But the golden rule won the day: if you do not want to be coerced in matters of faith, then extend that same freedom to others with whom you disagree.

Current Seventh-day Adventist General Conference President Ted N. C. Wilson summarized the concept underlying the First Amendment:

The core idea was that America should be a land where believers could practice their faith, free of government interference. But the other side of the coin is that those who don't believe also were to be free from legislative imperatives to follow the church's dictates.[89]

To some, the idea of separation of church and state seems unholy, but as Kramnick and Moore so aptly observe:

The creation of a godless constitution was not an act of irreverence. Far from it. It was an act of confidence in religion. It intended to let religion do what it did best, to preserve the civil morality necessary to democracy, without laying upon it the burdens of being tied to the fortunes of this or that political faction The godless Constitution must be understood as part of the American system of voluntary church support that has proved

---

88 Ibid., p. 151.
89 Ted N. C. Wilson, "Keeping Church at Arm's Length From State," *Huffpost,* https://www.huffpost.com/entry/keeping-church-at-arms-le_b_4226809?guccounter=1&guce_referrer=aHR0cHM-6Ly93d3cuZ29vZ2xlLmNvbS88&guce_referrer_sig=AQAAABI3c0k7gCrrMeT-jSk8O-gTjbDt2e-jC4FQ1OCRieAZBCh9cVg3Fw4kPHSBOqOgkbNCuZOePGFlKCdkZbBO_p2ag-cXecPYdmld-0WJIP4BCyN4zQ9GZeyfNdedX26qpyH9KNnmfndwqGTkj9vOyCOFEXir46rPgFlbwmCPnfFMml

itself a much greater boon to the fortunes of organized religion than the prior systems of church establishment ever were.[90]

PUBLIC MORALITY VS. PRIVATE MORALITY

How then do we reconcile the principle that Christians ought to be involved in making society a better place by voting for, in White's words, "temperance and virtue" with the idea of separation of church and state? While the Bible offers no support for those who wish to enforce their *religion* on others in a secular society, followers of Jesus are called to be salt and light in the world. Consequently, their influence should tell on the side of truth, justice, and virtue. And that includes how they vote and participate in civil society.

Rejecting an overtly religious law is easy. But what about laws that seek to regulate individual or societal morality – where should we draw the line? Francis D. Nichol, longtime editor of *The Review and Herald*, articulated a useful standard:

I cannot see how we, as champions of religious liberty, can safely enter into the discussion of laws at all unless we ever *hold to the clear-cut principle that civil statutes must be built upon and defended by civil reasons.* This, of course, does not say for a moment that various civil prohibitory laws, such as those against murder, robbery, and so forth, are not also found in the Good Book. It means that if we are going to avoid confusing the realm of the religious and the civil, we must find a sufficient justification on civil grounds for these various statutes, altogether apart from any Biblical arguments.[91]

Former President Barack Obama, writing as a senator, articulated this same principle in a 2006 op-ed for *USA Today*, writing

90 Kramnick and Moore, p. 24.
91 Francis D. Nichol, *Answers to Objections* (Washington, D.C.: Review and Herald Pub. Assn., 1952), p. 858.

that "My faith shapes my values, but applying those values to policymaking *must be done with principles that are accessible to all people, religious or not.* Even so, those who enter the public square are not required to leave their beliefs at the door."[92] Christians should have a voice in society. But, as Nichol points out, they should advocate for social justice and public morality based on principles that they can justify based "on civil grounds…altogether apart from any Biblical arguments."

IS THERE A PLACE FOR LAWS ENFORCING MORALITY?

It's important to define what we mean by religion and morality. Religion has to do with our worship or allegiance to a deity; morality is concerned with correct human behavior. Almost everyone agrees that certain moral standards are essential for a functioning society. The prohibitions against murder and child pornography are based on morality. Likewise, enforcing laws against theft and robbery is the enforcement of morality. The sticking point is when it comes to laws enforcing an aspect of morality that the larger culture no longer deems important or a moral standard that is only considered such because of its status as a religious conviction.

In the words of Nichol, Christians "must find a sufficient justification on civil grounds for [laws enforcing morality], altogether apart from any Biblical arguments." Another useful tool that clarifies which moral principles should be made into laws and which should be left to individual conscience is the distinction between *public morality* and *private morality*. For our purposes, public morality can be defined as a behavior that somehow harms other people (i.e., the public), while private morality can be defined as a behavior that causes no direct harm to society and therefore

92 Barack Obama, "Politicians Need Not Abandon Religion," *USA Today*, July 10, 2006, http://usatoday.printthis.clickability.com/pt/cpt?action=cpt&title=Pol...n%2Feditorials%2F2006-07-09-forum-religion-obama_x.htm&partnerID=1660.

should be left to individual conscience or preference. Public morality can legitimately be regulated by the state, while the state would be overstepping its bounds to regulate private morality.

Marriage between a man and a woman is a good example. Christians fall on both sides of the debate when it comes to whether heterosexual marriage ought to be the law of the land. From a biblical and theological standpoint, God's ideal for marriage is what He created it to be in the book of Genesis: a lifelong, monogamous commitment between one man and one woman.[93] But should those who believe in God's plan for marriage enforce this ideal on the rest of society? It is beyond the scope of this book to argue one way or the other. But a good question to ask is this: Does same-sex marriage harm the public? In arguing whether it does or does not, Christians, in the words

---

93 On a theological level, the issues of same-sex relationships and abortion generate much discussion. Of course, when it comes to sin, God's foremost concern seems to be with the sins of His church. For example, Jesus declared to Capernaum, a city where He had repeatedly given evidence of His divinity, that "if the deeds of power done in you had been done in Sodom, it would have remained until this day. But I tell you that on the day of judgment it will be more tolerable for the land of Sodom than for you." (Matthew 11:23-24, NRSV). Sodom was known for its sexual perversion (see, e.g., Jude 7). Jesus also told the Pharisees that Nineveh, the city known for violence and bloodshed, would be better off in the day of judgment than their own kind. (See Matthew 12:41). Pagan Nineveh's moral awakening to social justice, although apparently short-lived, was more commendable than the legalistic moral correctness of the ostensibly righteous Pharisees.

Which is not to say that the sins of Sodom and Nineveh didn't matter; they did and they do. The Bible doesn't leave much doubt that sex outside of marriage, as God instituted it in Eden, is sin – whether that sex is heterosexual or homosexual. The same is true for the shedding of innocent blood. Yet for Christians, Jesus seems to be telling us to "first take the log out of your own eye, and then you will see clearly to take the speck out of your neighbor's eye." (Matthew 7:3-5, NRSV). Speaking to believers, Paul asked a pointed question: "You that boast in the law, do you dishonor God by breaking the law?" And then he issued a scathing rebuke: "For, as it is written, 'The name of God is blasphemed among the Gentiles because of you.'" (Romans 2:23-24, NRSV). White weighed in with this sobering reminder to the church of today: "The Redeemer of the world declares that there are greater sins than that for which Sodom and Gomorrah were destroyed. Those who hear the gospel invitation calling sinners to repentance, and heed it not, are more guilty before God than were the dwellers in the vale of Siddim. And still greater sin is theirs who profess to know God and to keep His commandments, yet who deny Christ in their character and their daily life. In the light of the Saviour's warning, the fate of Sodom is a solemn admonition, not merely to those who are guilty of outbreaking sin, but to all who are trifling with Heaven-sent light and privileges." (Ellen G. White, *Patriarchs and Prophets*, p. 165).

Should God's people speak up about sex outside of marriage and abortion? Yes, but with humility – and with the realization that we have many sins within our own camp that rival those of society around us.

of Francis D. Nichol, ought to "find sufficient justification on civil grounds" and should not simply seek to force their will on society at large "because the Bible says so."

Abortion is another area where public morality may be at stake. Abortion is a terrible and traumatic event for everyone involved. As a social issue, abortion is unique because there are at least two potential liberty interests at issue: 1) the liberty interest of the unborn child and 2) the liberty interest of the mother who is carrying the unborn child in her womb. To simply outlaw all abortions may not take into account the mother's liberty interest. To simply ignore it may not take into account the liberty interest of the unborn child.

Does abortion harm the public? One side would argue that it most definitely does – that life begins at the moment of conception and any harm to the unborn child, at any stage of development, should be outlawed, and the abortion provider (and/or mother) prosecuted for murder. Those on the other end of the spectrum would argue that abortion does not necessarily harm the general public, and that it is merely a private issue between the mother and her doctor. A third group would argue that at some early stage of development the zygote or embryo is a potential – but not necessarily a fully-formed – human being. They would note, however, that at some point in its development the unborn child should be afforded civil rights, and at that point in time the abortion of the unborn child would become an issue of public morality.[94] From a theological standpoint, Christians can all hopefully agree that the voluntary termination of a pregnancy, if not always a sin itself, is at least a byproduct of living in a sinful world. On a public policy level, Christians ought to agree that being pro-life in the real world means more than merely outlawing abortions. Followers of Jesus should also try to

---

94 Sean Pitman, M.D., has written an insightful piece that illustrates the complexity of this issue from a Christian perspective: "Updating the Seventh-day Adventist Position on Abortion" which can be found at: https://www.educatetruth.com/featured/updating-the-sda-position-on-abortion/.

understand what drives a woman to seek an abortion. Ultimately, Christians should advocate for public policies that will actually decrease the demand for abortions, including accountability for the men responsible for causing unwanted pregnancies that lead to abortions.

It is unfortunate that American Christians have, for the most part, become known as being "anti-abortion" but not necessarily "pro-life" in areas other than abortion. Conservative American Christianity is not usually known for being pro-life when it comes to making contraception free and easily accessible, supporting government aid for poor mothers who are most likely to seek an abortion, or supporting government food and medical programs for the children of those impoverished mothers. But regardless of where Christians land on the issue of abortion or gay marriage, they should argue for laws "with principles that are accessible to all people, religious or not," and not merely seek to legislate the Bible as the law of the land.

Kramnick and Moore's succinct summary says it well:

> We believe that in a democratic society abortion advocates and abortion foes can legitimately and passionately debate the issue in the political arenas where public policy is crafted, be they legislative, administrative, or judicial. In these debates moral and religious convictions will and should play a prominent part. *What is unacceptable…in light of the godless Constitution is for religious certainty ever to trump politics and for government policy in any way to privilege or codify religious belief in ways that preempt a pluralist democratic process.* Public policies in the United States must never be put to a litmus test of religious correctness.[95]

In relation to the discussion of private and public morality, Christians should consider the important distinction to be made

---

95 Kramnick and Moore, p. 176.

between laws that simply *allow* immoral behavior and laws that *compel* people to disobey the law of God. Wilson asks:

> Will government ever make laws with which we as a church strongly disagree? Yes, absolutely. Like many other faiths, the Seventh-day Adventist church subscribes to the Biblical definition of marriage as being between a man and a woman, for example. But where we differ from some of our peers is that we acknowledge that there's a difference between government allowing certain actions with which we might disagree on moral grounds…as opposed to compelling them. That is the fine line that is religious liberty.[96]

Wilson seems to be making a distinction that applies especially to private morality. Christians ought to be cautious to advocate for outlawing behavior simply because it is unbiblical, unless that behavior can also be shown to be harmful to the public at large. Even if a behavior can be shown to harm the public, Christians should advocate for public morality using "principles that are accessible to all people, religious or not."[97]

A TIME FOR PROTEST AND CIVIL DISOBEDIENCE

Advocating for public morality has often taken the form of public protest. The ancient prophets protested against oppressive government, with Isaiah writing: "Woe to those who make unjust laws, to those who issue oppressive decrees, to deprive the poor of their rights and withhold justice from the oppressed of my people" (Isaiah 10:1–2, NIV).

In America, protest has often been a part of nudging the needle of justice toward better laws. Government can be used by God to protect the oppressed, but it can also be the source of

---

96 Wilson, "Keeping Church at Arm's Length from State."
97 Obama, "Politicians Need Not Abandon Religion."

oppression and evil itself. Christians should understand that there are appropriate times and circumstances for civil disobedience. While the Apostle Peter admonished his listeners, "Submit yourselves for the Lord's sake to every human authority: whether to the emperor, as the supreme authority, or to governors, who are sent by him to punish those who do wrong and to commend those who do right" (1 Peter 2:13–14, NIV), it was Peter who also proclaimed to the authorities, "We must obey God rather than human beings!" (Acts 5:29, NIV). Like Shadrach, Meshach, and Abednego, who obeyed the king's order to appear at the dedication of the image, yet refused to worship that same image, Christians ought to comply with human laws to the extent that those laws do not cause them to violate the law of God.

In the spring of 1963, Martin Luther King Jr. led out in coordinated peaceful protests against state-sponsored segregation and racism in Birmingham, Alabama. King was jailed for participating in the protest. Confined to the Birmingham city jail and under harsh conditions, King wrote his famous "Letter from a Birmingham Jail." It was a response to criticism against King from local white pastors. In the letter, he eloquently articulated the conditions under which Christians can and should participate in civil disobedience.

> You express a great deal of anxiety over our willingness to break laws. This is certainly a legitimate concern. Since we so diligently urge people to obey the Supreme Court's decision of 1954 outlawing segregation in the public schools, at first glance it may seem rather paradoxical for us consciously to break laws. One may well ask: "How can you advocate breaking some laws and obeying others?" The answer lies in the fact that there are two types of laws: just and unjust. I would be the first to advocate obeying just laws. One has not only a legal but a moral responsibility to obey just laws. Conversely, one has a moral responsibility to disobey unjust laws. I would agree with St. Augustine that "an unjust law is no law at all."

Now, what is the difference between the two? How does one determine whether a law is just or unjust? A just law is a man-made code that squares with the moral law or the law of God. An unjust law is a code that is out of harmony with the moral law. To put it in the terms of St. Thomas Aquinas: An unjust law is a human law that is not rooted in eternal law and natural law. Any law that uplifts human personality is just. Any law that degrades human personality is unjust. All segregation statutes are unjust because segregation distorts the soul and damages the personality. It gives the segregator a false sense of superiority and the segregated a false sense of inferiority… Thus it is that I can urge men to obey the 1954 decision of the Supreme Court, for it is morally right; and I can urge them to disobey segregation ordinances, for they are morally wrong.[98]

As noted earlier, White also advocated for civil disobedience using a similar theological framework as King. In the context of the Fugitive Slave Act of 1850, which required escaped slaves to be returned to their enslavers, White wrote the following:

Where the laws of men conflict with God's word and law, we are to obey the word and law of God, whatever the consequences may be. The laws of our land requiring us to deliver a slave to his master, we are not to obey, and we must abide the consequences of the violation of this law.[99]

IT'S ABOUT DOING JUSTICE

The Bible commands us to "[s]peak up for those who cannot speak for themselves, for the rights of all who are destitute. Speak up and judge fairly; defend the rights of the poor and needy" (Proverbs 31:8–9, NIV). The Bible also reminds us that the

---

98 Martin Luther King Jr., "Letter from a Birmingham Jail," https://www.africa.upenn.edu/Articles_Gen/Letter_Birmingham.html.
99 Ellen G. White, *Spiritual Gifts*, vol. 4b, p. 42.

kingdom of God is "not of this world" (John 18:36) and that we are not called to fight to establish His kingdom on earth. Consequently, Christians and non-Christians alike should seek common ground on issues of social justice and public morality and should work toward a common goal of making a more just and fair society for all people while carefully avoiding any attempt to establish the kingdom of God on earth through the legislation of religion that Ellen G. White and others warned against.

On an individual level, it's up to us as followers of Jesus to surrender to the power of the Holy Spirit so that we will live by the principles of the Bible. God will then use us to share His good news with others, and this ripple effect will, little by little, transform individuals and society at large. Ellen White put it this way:

> If the teachings of God's word were made the controlling influence in the life of every man and woman, if mind and heart were brought under its restraining power, the evils that now exist in national and in social life would find no place. *From every home would go forth an influence* that would make men and women strong in spiritual insight and in moral power, and thus nations and individuals would be placed on vantage ground.[100]

For believers, doing justice originates in the heart. When the principles of the Bible inform the choices and actions, doing justice will be the natural result. While followers of Jesus will work for a more just and fair society, they will never consent to forced religion. Instead, they will use their influence to advocate for public morality, including laws that benefit the poor and those experiencing discrimination and oppression, while simultaneously defending freedom of conscience for believers and nonbelievers alike in matters of faith.

---

100 Ellen G. White, *Prophets and Kings*, p. 192, https://egwwritings.org.

TAKE ACTION: DO JUSTICE NOW

- What is a specific cause that I will adopt to seek justice for the oppressed?

- How can I use my voice and vote to advocate for public virtue and morality, liberty of conscience, and the separation of church and state?

*"Then Jesus said to them,
Give back to Caesar
what is Caesar's and to
God what is God's"*

MARK 12:17, NIV

CHAPTER SIX

AMERICAN RELIGION AT THE END

Back to our imaginary island where the Ten Commandments are the law of the land. On this island, you are required to attend religious services, and compliance is strictly enforced. The idea is that moral people make good citizens, and church attendance helps make people moral. As a nod to democracy, the islanders are able to elect their leaders, provided that only church members in good and regular standing are eligible to hold political office.

On the island, those who dissent against the prevailing religious views are punished harshly – with imprisonment, deportation, torture, or death. The prevailing wisdom is that dissent against morality and spirituality is ultimately harmful to society and must be stamped out. All islanders are required to support the state church with their tax dollars so the religious leaders can focus their full energies on making the island's citizens moral and good.

Are you ready to move to the island?

Believe it or not, something similar took place in Puritan colonial America! In Salem, Massachusetts, for example, the leaders set about creating a government that "would be based upon laws which in all causes would follow the rule of God's word."[101] That led to the devout Christian citizens of Salem executing a

---

101 Barry, p. 109.

Christian minister, Pastor George Burroughs, because he was suspected of being a witch.

Borroughs was an odd and a somewhat secretive person. Besides allegations of superhuman strength (it was rumored that he could lift a musket with one finger), he could not remember the last time he had partaken in the Lord's Supper, and there were indications that he did not believe in the prevailing orthodox position on infant baptism.[102] There were more allegations, to be sure, but they all seemed to be based on accusations of some of Boroughs' former parishioners who had sued him for debt.

At his execution, Borroughs gave such an eloquent and sincere speech that some of the spectators began to weep, and the officials were worried that some might try to hinder his execution. Nevertheless, George Burroughs was executed by hanging and then unceremoniously cut down and dragged to a shallow grave, where he was buried.[103]

Of this era in early American history, where the church controlled the state, Ellen G. White would write:

The regulation adopted by the early colonists, of permitting only members of the church to vote or to hold office in the civil government, led to most pernicious results. This measure had been accepted as a means of preserving the purity of the state, but it resulted in the corruption of the church. A profession of religion being the condition of suffrage and officeholding, many, actuated solely by motives of worldly policy, united with the church without a change of heart. Thus the churches came to consist, to a considerable extent, of unconverted persons; and even in the ministry were those who not only held errors of doctrine, but who were ignorant of the renewing power of the Holy Spirit. Thus again was demonstrated the evil results,

---

102 Rebecca Beatrice Brooks, "The Witchcraft Trial of Reverend George Burroughs," https://historyofmassachusetts.org/reverend-george-burroughs-salem/.
103 "George Burroughs," https://en.wikipedia.org/wiki/George_Burroughs.

so often witnessed in the history of the church from the days of Constantine to the present, of attempting to build up the church by the aid of the state, of appealing to the secular power in support of the gospel of Him who declared: "My kingdom is not of this world." John 18:36. *The union of the church with the state, be the degree never so slight, while it may appear to bring the world nearer to the church, does in reality but bring the church nearer to the world.*[104]

Keep in mind that George Burrough's persecutors were not necessarily outwardly evil people. Many of them were no doubt devout Christians who considered themselves followers of Jesus. And no surprise, for a "blind zeal under false religious theories is the most violent and merciless."[105] In fact, it was some of the original Christians – the disciples James and John – who at one point asked Jesus for permission to destroy a village of Samaritans who had refused to welcome Him. Jesus' response to these "sons of thunder" teaches us something vitally important: that as His disciples, we have no place in forcing acceptance of Jesus – or mere outward behavioral changes in the name of Jesus – on others. Jesus' words remind us that He respected the free choice of even those who rejected Him. "He turned and rebuked them, and said, 'You do not know what manner of spirit you are of. For the Son of Man did not come to destroy men's lives but to save them'" (Luke 9:55–56, NKJV).

Speaking of events to take place in the world prior to His second coming, Jesus said:

All this I have told you so that you will not fall away. They will put you out of the synagogue; *in fact, the time is coming when anyone who kills you will think they are offering a service to God. They will do such things because they have not known the Father or me* (John 16:1–3, NIV).

---

104 Ellen G. White, *The Great Controversy*, p. 297.
105 Ellen G. White, *The Southern Work*, p. 74.

In other words, Jesus is telling us that at least some of the end-time persecutors will be professed Christians – sincere in their misguided attempts to force others. What leads them to do these things? Jesus said it will be "because they have not known the Father or me." Essentially, a counterfeit version of Jesus will become popular in religious circles. This false Christ will have no problem with coercion in matters of faith and will blend patriotism with worship to the point where they become one and the same.

THE UNITED STATES IN PROPHECY

> Then I saw another beast coming up out of the earth, and he had two horns like a lamb and spoke like a dragon. And he exercises all the authority of the first beast in his presence, and causes the earth and those who dwell in it to worship the first beast, whose deadly wound was healed (Revelation 13:11–12, NKJV).

A beast is symbolic of a kingdom, nation, or political entity in apocalyptic prophecy (Daniel 7:17). Here, Revelation describes an end-time nation with worldwide reach and influence. Also note that this second beast-nation of Revelation 13 has "two horns like a lamb" and speaks "like a dragon." The Lamb in Revelation symbolizes Jesus (see Revelation 5:6; 12:11, etc.), and so this superpower nation must have some Christ-like characteristics. But don't forget the second part – it speaks like the dragon. Who is the dragon in Revelation? Revelation 12:9 tells us that the dragon represents "that serpent of old, called the Devil and Satan, who deceives the whole world" (NKJV).

Many Bible students have understood this second nation to symbolize the United States of America. In the 1800s, Seventh-day Adventists noted that America was already speaking like a dragon as the nation enslaved and brutalized African

Americans.[106] But Revelation 13 predicted more: that this second nation would cause "the earth and those who dwell in it to worship the first beast" and tell "those who dwell on the earth to make an image to the beast" (Revelation 13:12, 14, NKJV). From this symbolism, Adventists saw the United States abandoning its Lamb-like characteristics, namely, civil and religious liberty. Freedom to worship (or not worship), as protected by the First Amendment, would no longer be respected in America, and a new form of government would be created.

Notice that the Bible indicates that the government will appeal to the people to "make an image" of the first beast-nation. This appeal to the citizenry indicates some sort of a representative form of government that you find in a democracy. In this scenario, the people of the United States – through their representatives – would then create a copy – an image – of the first nation mentioned in Revelation 13. Many Protestants historically have understood the first beast-nation of Revelation to be the medieval Roman church. That church is unique in that it is both a church and a sovereign state – *a union of a church and state.*

But shouldn't we want church and state to be united, with religious leaders having our favorite politician's ear? With the decline of morals in society, don't we want to make sure that only Christians hold political office? Why not make the Bible the law of the land and have government-led prayer in schools?[107]

---

106 See, e.g., Trevor O'Reggio's article, "Slavery, Prophecy, and the American Nation as Seen by the Adventist Pioneers, 1854–1865," https://digitalcommons.andrews.edu/cgi/viewcontent.cgi?article=1184&context=jats.

107 The issue of government-led prayer is a difficult one. On one hand, public servants ought to be allowed to speak freely about their faith in the public square. On the other hand, government officials should be careful not to coerce others in matters of faith, including by forcing the public to participate in prayer. White comments on King Nebuchadnezzar's public confession of faith in Daniel 3:28–29 by noting that "[i]t was right for the king to make public confession, and to seek to exalt the God of heaven above all other gods; but in endeavoring to force his subjects to make a similar confession of faith and to show similar reverence, Nebuchadnezzar was exceeding his right as a temporal sovereign. He had no more right, either civil or moral, to threaten men with death for not worshiping God, than he had to make the decree consigning to the flames all who refused to worship the golden image. God never compels the obedience of man. He leaves all free to choose whom they will serve." (Ellen G. White, *Prophets and Kings*, p. 511). The Church State Council has published a pamphlet by Pastor James

The story of the early Adventist believers gives us nuanced but clear answers to these questions. While Adventists were involved in social issues and seeking justice for their neighbor, their understanding of apocalyptic prophecy led them to strenuously oppose the church grasping of the reins of political power to enforce religion.

WHY WILL THIS HAPPEN?

So what could lead Americans to effectively repudiate the principle of separation of church and state found in our Constitution? Perhaps the citizens of the United States, the vast majority of whom still claim to be Christian, will forget that Jesus never forces people to serve Him. Like James and John, they will embrace a false version of Jesus that seeks to destroy those who reject Him, forgetting that "God never compels the obedience of man. He leaves all free to choose whom they will serve."[108] Perhaps people will then unite to combat the increasing secularism and immorality they see in America. Perhaps, as natural and man-made disasters increase, even secular Americans will seek a religious-political solution to the world's problems. As in Christ's day, when both the conservative Pharisees and the liberal Sadducees put aside their differences to crucify their common enemy and avert a potential political crisis, the various religious and political factions in America will unite to solve a common problem. The next step would be to establish a government that is a union of church and state. Even today, we hear rumblings of it more and more from the religious-political warriors of today, who are no doubt sincere in their desire to raise the moral standard in the world.

Once again, White saw a backslidden Christian church as being the underlying cause:

L. Evans, entitled *In the Fight for Public Prayer, Prayer Suffers*, which provides a unique perspective on the topic of government-led prayer.
108 Ellen G. White, *Prophets and Kings*, p. 511.

Finding herself destitute of the power of love, [the church] has reached out for the strong arm of the state to enforce her dogmas and execute her decrees. Here is the secret of all religious laws that have ever been enacted, and *the secret of all persecution from the days of Abel to our own time.*[109]

White then explained exactly how she saw this happening in America. In her monumental work, *The Great Controversy*, she wrote: "In order for the United States to form an image of the beast, *the religious power must so control the civil government* that the authority of the state will also be employed by the church to accomplish her own ends."[110]

When the Protestant churches shall unite with the secular power to sustain a false religion…; *when the state shall use its power to enforce the decrees and sustain the institutions of the church* – then will Protestant America have formed an image to the papacy, [a church-state union].[111]

Notice that White predicted that *the church* would be controlling the government, and the state would use its power to enforce the decrees of *the church.*

Revelation foretells the great harlot, symbolizing a revived medieval church, committing spiritual fornication with the end-time political powers. (See Revelation 17:1–2.) The harlot (the church) rides the beast (the political entities), indicating that the church plays a dominant role over the state at the end of time. But why does the Bible call this union between the church and the kings of the earth "fornication"? Because God considers this intimate relationship between church and state to be sinful. And it's not just the kings of the earth who will be in bed with

---

109 Ellen G. White, *Thoughts from the Mount of Blessing*, p. 127.

110 Ellen G. White, *The Great Controversy*, p. 443.

111 Francis D. Nichol, ed., *The Seventh-day Adventist Bible Commentary*, vol. 7 (Washington, D.C.: Review and Herald Pub. Assn., 1957), p. 976.

the apostate church. The prophecy says that "the inhabitants of the earth were made drunk with the wine of her fornication" (Revelation 17:2, NKJV), meaning, the whole Christian world experiences spiritual intoxication and comes to believe that this marriage of church and state is God's will.

LOVE, NOT FORCE

While Christians will be active in promoting justice for the poor and oppressed and improving the morals of society, they will simultaneously oppose using the Bible as a legislative bludgeon to coerce people into becoming religious. In fact, White noted that the impulse to force others in matters of faith originates with Satan. "There can be no more conclusive evidence that we possess the spirit of Satan than *the disposition to hurt and destroy those who do not appreciate our work, or who act contrary to our ideas.*"[112]

In the beginning when the world was perfect, when there was no sin or sadness, pain or death, God put a tree of choice in the garden: the tree of knowledge of good and evil. Why did he put that tree there? Because He is love and does not force the conscience. Among all the inducements to do right, God gave Adam and Eve the option of rejecting Him, because love – in order to be love – doesn't force itself upon others. *That tree was the freedom to sin.* Because love does to others what it would have done to itself, even at great risk of rejection or loss.

But is force always wrong?

A ROLE FOR COERCION

In a sinful world, God also recognizes that most people won't live by the golden rule. While it is never appropriate for governments to coerce in matters of faith or worship, there *is* a role for government coercion to protect the vulnerable in society.

---

112 Ellen G. White, *The Desire of Ages,* p. 487.

In Romans 13, the Apostle Paul outlines the role that "the sword," used by the civil magistrate, is to play:

- Government exists to protect people from harm by others.
- It is completely appropriate for earthly governments to (proportionally) punish crimes that people commit against people.

Christians ought to be on the forefront of advocating for government protections for all who are oppressed in society, including defending those who are oppressed by religious persecution. Christians ought to work to ensure that their government is not oppressive. Christians should seek a moral and just government that protects the civil rights and liberties of all people – those who believe and those who choose not to believe. In protecting the rights of the oppressed, Christians recognize that government may legitimately exercise force as a means of restraining the oppressor. But when it comes to building up the spiritual kingdom of God and the church, Jesus noted that His followers are not called to build *His kingdom* with "the sword" – i.e., earthly force. "My kingdom," Jesus said, "is not of this world. If My kingdom were of this world, then My servants would be fighting so that I would not be handed over to the Jews; but as it is, My kingdom is not of this realm" (John 18:36, NASB).

Along these lines, White said the following:

> To protect liberty of conscience is the duty of the state, and this is the limit of its authority in matters of religion. Every secular government that attempts to regulate or enforce religious observances by civil authority is sacrificing the very principle for which the evangelical Christians so nobly struggled.[113]

---

113 Ellen G. White, *The Great Controversy*, p. 201.

LOVE REQUIRES FREEDOM

Why shouldn't Christians want the government enforcing worship and religion? Because God desires only voluntary worship. He wants a love-based relationship with His creatures, and it's not true love if you have no choice in the matter.

Freedom ultimately brings with it incredible risk. While free choice brings unlimited possibilities to do good, it also includes the freedom to sin and to tear the universe apart. All the pain, sorrow, evil, and persecution experienced in this world stemmed from one act of disobedience at the tree in the Garden of Eden. But God's answer was another tree – the Cross of Jesus. God's Son would be lifted up, and there, between heaven and earth, Jesus would die because He'd rather die than take away our freedom of choice!

In the first tree, a satanic serpent deceived our first parents. On another tree, Jesus became sin itself, so that we could go free. "As Moses lifted up the serpent in the wilderness, so must the Son of Man be lifted up, so that everyone who believes will have eternal life in Him" (John 3:14–15, NASB). We rejected Him at one tree, but He accepted us at the other.

Shane Claiborne writes:

I believe in a God of scandalous grace. If I believed terrorists were beyond redemption, I would need to rip out half of my New Testament Scriptures, for they were written by a converted terrorist. I have pledged allegiance to a King who loved evildoers so much He died for them…teaching us that there is something worth dying for but nothing worth killing for. While terrorists were nailing Him to the cross, my Jesus pleaded that they be shown mercy for they [knew not] what they were doing. We are all wretched, and we are all beautiful. No one is beyond redemption…May we see in the hands of the oppressors our own hands, and in the faces of the oppressed, our own faces. We are made of the same dust, and we cry the same salty tears.[114]

This is a God who does not force people to worship Him but instead lays down His scourged and bloody body on a cross, His flesh gouged to the bone by the Roman whip. Here is a God with nails driven through His hands and feet who then prays for His Father to forgive His persecutors. This is the God of the Bible, not the counterfeit Jesus of the end-time persecutors. This God will convert the most hardened jihadist, persecutor, atheist, or skeptic – and even the most nominal Christian.

WHO CAN SAVE AMERICA?

Our world's problems won't be fixed by politicians who promise to bring America "back to God." Why? Because, while government exists to defend the oppressed, it's not the government's job to bring people to God. *Jesus actually wants His church to be His agent on earth to show the world who He really is.*

Followers of Jesus are to be on the forefront of alleviating suffering and injustice in the world (see, e.g., Matthew 25:31–46), but their goal isn't to set up an earthly version of God's kingdom on earth, to "enforce what they regarded as the laws of God, and to make [themselves] the expositors of His will and the agents of His authority." Because, while Christians will advocate for moral and just civil laws, they will also recognize that *religious* laws aren't the answer, and that Christ's kingdom will only be established "by the implanting of Christ's nature in humanity through the work of the Holy Spirit."[115] Only Jesus can ultimately save America – and the world. And He'll do it one person at a time, by showing His love and truth through you and me as we do justly, love mercy, and walk humbly with Him (Micah 6:8).

---

114 Shane Claiborne, "I'm going to Iraq," http://www.jmm.org.au/articles/18890.htm.
115 Ellen G. White, *The Desire of Ages*, p. 509.

TAKE ACTION: DO JUSTICE NOW

- How can I better understand and appreciate the love that God has for me?

- What are three concrete ways that I can share with others what the grace of God has done in my life?

- I can support justice for the oppressed while respecting the principle of separation of church and state by advocating for the following social and public policy issues:

"The Lord Jesus demands our acknowledgement of the rights of every man. Men's social rights, and their rights as Christians, are to be taken into consideration. All are to be treated with refinement and delicacy, as the sons and daughters of God"

E. G. WHITE,
GOSPEL WORKERS, P. 123

CHAPTER SEVEN

BIBLICAL SOCIAL JUSTICE AND THE THREE ANGELS' MESSAGES

Contrary to popular evangelical thought, religion will be on the ascendency at the end of time. John the Revelator predicted that the second beast-nation would make "the earth and its inhabitants *worship*" the first beast-nation and would tell the world "to make an image" – an imitation – of the first beast-nation's form of government, a combination of church and state (Revelation 13:12, 14).

The Apostle Paul further predicted that

There will be terrible times in the last days.
People will be lovers of themselves, lovers of money, boastful, proud, abusive, disobedient to their parents, ungrateful, unholy, without love, unforgiving, slanderous, without self-control, brutal, not lovers of the good, treacherous, rash, conceited, lovers of pleasure rather than lovers of God – *having a form of godliness but denying its power* (2 Timothy 3:1–5, NIV).

The prophet Isaiah described a form of religion that includes enthusiastic worship and even daily religious rituals but lacks genuine godly power.

Day after day they seek me and delight to know my ways, as if they were a nation that practiced righteousness and did not forsake the ordinance of their God; they ask of me righteous judgments, they delight to draw near to God. "Why do we fast, but you do not see? Why humble ourselves, but you do not notice?" (Isaiah 58:2–3, NRSV).

What could be missing from this religious experience? In one word: justice. Like the Pharisees of Jesus' day, these are religious people who fast and pray, have daily devotions, attend church, and pay tithe, but they have "neglected the more important matters of the law – *justice, mercy and faithfulness*" (Matthew 23:23, NIV).

The prophet Amos recorded God's shocking reaction to this empty worship:

I hate, I despise your religious festivals; your assemblies are a stench to me…Away with the noise of your songs! I will not listen to the music of your harps. But let justice roll on like a river, righteousness like a never-failing stream! (Amos 5:21, 23–24, NIV).

THE ANTIDOTE TO EMPTY RELIGION

What's the solution to this empty form of godliness? Isaiah tells us:

Is not this the fast that I choose: to loose the bonds of injustice, to undo the thongs of the yoke, to let the oppressed go free, and to break every yoke? Is it not to share your bread with the hungry, and bring the homeless poor into your house; when you see the naked, to cover them, and not to hide yourself from your own kin? (Isaiah 58:6–7, NRSV).

Some may argue that Isaiah's words now apply only in a spiritual sense – to freeing people from spiritual oppression. But Ellen G. White certainly didn't see it that way. Writing to a church member in defense of a *Review and Herald* article condemning racism and bigotry toward Blacks, White wrote:

> Why not cut out of your Bibles [the passage where] Christ refers to His work, "The Spirit of the Lord God is upon Me; because He hath anointed Me to preach good tidings unto the meek; he hath sent me to bind up the brokenhearted, to proclaim liberty to the captives, and the opening of the prison to them that are bound" (Isaiah 61:1)?[116]

In another place, White wrote:

> I have been instructed to refer our people to the fifty-eighth chapter of Isaiah. Read this chapter carefully, and understand the kind of ministry that will bring life into the churches. The work of the gospel is to be carried by means of our liberality as well as by our labors. When you meet suffering souls who need help, give it to them. When you find those who are hungry, feed them. In doing this you will be working in lines of Christ's ministry.[117]

White also emphasized that the work of relieving literal oppression should go hand in hand with relieving spiritual oppression:

> I have no fears of workers who are engaged in the work represented in the fifty-eighth chapter of Isaiah. This chapter is explicit, and is enough to enlighten any one who wishes to do the will of God. There is plenty of opportunity for everyone to be a blessing to humanity. *The third angel's message is not to be given a second place in this work, but is to be one with it.* There may be and there is a danger of burying up the great principles of truth when doing the work that is right to do. This work is to be to

---

116 Ellen G. White, *Letter 36, 1880*, par. 6.
117 Ellen G. White, *Ministry to the Cities*, p. 56, https://egwwritings.org.

the message as the hand is to the body. The spiritual necessities of the soul are to be kept prominent.[118]

At the same time, White cautioned against focusing entirely on working for, in her words, "the poorer classes," writing that

> The work for the poorer classes has no limit. It can never be got through with, and it must be treated as a part of the great whole. To give our first attention to this work, while there are vast portions of the Lord's vineyard open to culture and yet untouched, is to begin in the wrong place. As the right arm is to the body, so is the medical missionary work to the third angel's message. But the right arm is not to become the whole body. The work of seeking the outcasts is important, but it is not to become the great burden of our mission.[119]

Yet, later, she had no hesitation in writing, "The whole of the fifty-eighth chapter of Isaiah is to be regarded as a message for this time, to be given over and over again."[120]

> A religion that would lead us to be careless of human needs, sufferings, or rights, is a spurious religion. In slighting the claims of the poor, the suffering, and the sinful, we are proving ourselves traitors to Christ...When those who profess the name of Christ shall practice the principles of the golden rule, the same power will attend the gospel as in apostolic times.[121]

BIBLICAL SOCIAL JUSTICE AND THE SABBATH

In reading Isaiah 58, one can't help but notice the reference to the Sabbath at the end of the chapter. How is the Sabbath

---

118 Ellen G. White, *Letter 24, 1898,* par. 4, https://egwwritings.org.
119 Ellen G. White, *Welfare Ministry,* p. 258.
120 Ibid., p. 29.
121 Ellen G. White, *Thoughts From the Mount of Blessing,* p. 137.

connected to biblical social justice? In reality, the two are inseparable. The "repairers of the breach" are the same people who are setting the oppressed free and breaking every yoke. (See Isaiah 58:6, 12.) In other words, genuine Sabbath keeping and working for biblical social justice go hand in hand.

The Sabbath command itself requires social justice. "Remember the Sabbath day, to keep it holy…In it you shall do no work: you, *nor your son, nor your daughter, nor your male servant, nor your female servant, nor your cattle, nor your stranger who is within your gates*" (Exodus 20:8–10, NKJV). The seventh-day Sabbath is not a day of self-centered rest. On the Sabbath, we rest, and we allow all others within our orbit to also rest. It is a day when everyone – employer and employee, rich and poor, producer and consumer – is treated equally and allowed to rest. "Six days you shall do your work, and on the seventh day you shall rest, that your ox and your donkey may rest, and the son of your female servant and the stranger may be refreshed" (Exodus 23:12, NKJV).

Right before Jesus returns in the clouds of heaven, an everlasting gospel is shared around the world. Revelation 14:6–12 describes the delivery of this message using the symbol of three angels flying around the world "to proclaim to those who live on the earth – to every nation, tribe, language and people" (Revelation 14:6, NIV). The first angel's message alludes to the Sabbath commandment: "Fear God and give him glory, because the hour of his judgment has come. Worship him who made the heavens, the earth, the sea and the springs of water" (verse 7). The phrase "made the heavens, the earth, the sea" points us back to the Sabbath commandment, with the very language of Exodus 20:11. In other words, God's end-time message will be calling people to worship Him on the day of rest that He made holy when He created the world. Those who respond to the everlasting gospel will "keep the commandments of God and hold fast to the faith of Jesus" (Revelation 14:12, NRSV).

But recall that correct worship is more than mere compliance with forms or rituals – or even observance of the correct day. Those who keep and proclaim the Sabbath at the end of time will be the same people doing justice in the world – the work of Isaiah 58. Those who are breaking every yoke and following Jesus by proclaiming liberty to the captives "shall be called the repairers of the breach" (Isaiah 58:12; 60:1–4). The message of the seventh day Sabbath, as contained in Isaiah 58, Revelation 14:7, and Exodus 20:8–11, is a message to do unto others as you would have them do to you. The purpose of the Sabbath is for God's people to exercise trust in Him (by keeping the right day, even if it may seem arbitrary) and build a relationship with Him (by spending time with Him). As they enter into His Sabbath rest, God reveals Himself to His people and writes in their hearts His law of other-centered love (Hebrews 8:10–13).

Those who keep the commandments of God, including the Sabbath commandment, stand in contrast to those who worship the beast-nation and receive its mark. The law of God is to be in the mind and heart of believers; the mark of the beast is a counterfeit, in that those who receive the mark of the beast-nation submit to a counterfeit version of God's law. The followers of the beast are the same as those described by Paul who have a "form of godliness" (2 Timothy 3:5), and as those described by Isaiah who seek God daily "as if they were a nation that practiced righteousness and did not forsake the ordinance of their God" (Isaiah 58:2, NRSV). Yet, these are the same people who have neglected to do justice for the poor and oppressed, and as a natural next step, they persecute the people of God who keep the commandments of God and are doing justice in the world. (See, e.g., John 16:1–3.) The Sabbath command to rest in God's forgiveness and love, and to extend that same mercy to others, is God's "seal" of His end-time people. It is the mark of those who are following in the footsteps of Jesus and proclaiming "liberty to the captives" like He did (Luke 4:18).

White agreed:

> I cannot too strongly urge all our church members, all who
> are true missionaries, all who believe the third angel's message,
> all who turn away their feet from the Sabbath, to consider
> the message of the fifty-eighth chapter of Isaiah. The work
> of beneficence enjoined in this chapter is the work that God
> requires His people to do at this time.[122]

> The fifty-eighth chapter of Isaiah contains present truth for the
> people of God. Here we see how medical missionary work and
> the gospel ministry are to be bound together as the message is
> given to the world. Upon those who keep the Sabbath of the
> Lord is laid the responsibility of doing a work of mercy and
> benevolence. Medical missionary work is to be bound up with
> the message, and sealed with the seal of God.[123]

For those who follow Jesus in doing justice in the world, there
are amazing promises:

> Then your light shall break forth like the dawn, and your
> healing shall spring up quickly, your vindicator shall go before
> you, the glory of the Lord shall be your rear guard. Then you
> shall call, and the Lord will answer; you shall cry for help, and
> he will say, Here I am…If you refrain from trampling the
> sabbath, from pursuing your own interests on my holy day;
> if you call the sabbath a delight and the holy day of the Lord
> honorable; if you honor it, not going your own ways, serving
> your own interests, or pursuing your own affairs; then you shall
> take delight in the Lord, and I will make you ride upon the
> heights of the earth; I will feed you with the heritage of your
> ancestor Jacob, for the mouth of the Lord has spoken (Isaiah
> 58:8–9, 13–14, NRSV).

---

122 Ellen G. White, *Testimonies for the Church*, vol. 6, p. 265, https://egwwritings.org.
123 Ellen G. White, *Evangelism*, pp. 516–517, https://egwwritings.org.

Ultimately, the story of the Sabbath and social justice is about salvation through Jesus. Like the Israelites who were saved in Egypt from destruction by the blood of the Lamb covering their homes, we are saved by the sacrifice of Jesus, the Lamb of God. Like the Israelites who passed through the Red Sea, we receive water baptism, a potent symbol of our death to the old slavery of sin and our new life in Christ. Then, like the Israelites, as we journey through the wilderness, we are made ready to enter the heavenly promised land. The first generation of Israelites did not enter the promised land because of their unbelief in the promises of God's grace and their subsequent disobedience (Hebrews 3:16–19).

Resting on the seventh day Sabbath is an act of trust in God. As we rest on God's weekly day of rest, we cease from our own misguided efforts to save ourselves and demonstrate faith in God's ability to save us and take us to heaven.

> So then, a sabbath rest still remains for the people of God; for those who enter God's rest also cease from their labors as God did from his. Let us therefore make every effort to enter that rest, so that no one may fall through such disobedience as theirs (Hebrews 4:9–11, NRSV).

When we enter into the rest of salvation in Jesus, trusting in His sacrifice to forgive our sins and believing He knows what is best for us, we will obey His commandments because He has written them in our heart (Hebrews 8:10–13; John 14:15; 1 John 2:3–6). As we enter into His rest, we have the heart of God and want to do the work He does. Instead of pursuing our own interests, we "call the sabbath a delight and the holy day of the Lord honorable" doing the work of loosing "the bonds of injustice," undoing "the thongs of the yoke, to let the oppressed go free," and breaking "every yoke" (Isaiah 58:13, 6, NRSV).

Doing justice leads to transformation in our own lives. The Bible calls it sanctification (Ezekiel 20:12). And this is why, at the final judgment, those who inherit the kingdom are the ones to whom Jesus says,

> I was hungry and you gave me food, I was thirsty and you gave me something to drink, I was a stranger and you welcomed me, I was naked and you gave me clothing, I was sick and you took care of me, I was in prison and you visited me (Matthew 25:35–36, NRSV).

The righteous respond that they didn't know they were doing these things to Jesus. In other words, they weren't doing these things to earn salvation or out of fear of punishment. Instead, they were doing these righteous acts because when one follows Jesus, it becomes natural to do justice. Why is doing justice for the least of these the litmus test for those who will inherit the kingdom? Because that's what heaven is like. It's a place where unselfish love is the reigning principle, and only those who live unselfishly will fit into heaven for eternity.

TAKE ACTION: DO JUSTICE NOW

- How can I know God better for who He truly is?

- How can I genuinely worship God in how I live my life?

- What are some ways that I can promote justice for the oppressed on the Sabbath day?

WHY THE WORLD NEEDS THE CHURCH NOW MORE THAN EVER

In Chapter 5 of this book, Kramnick and Moore reminded us of something important about American democracy.

A democratic government was not created to produce moral citizens. It was the other way around: moral citizens constructed and preserved democracy. The founders left the business of teaching morality to private concerns, a principle that should carry some weight with present-day conservatives.[124]

They then add:

It follows from this formulation that if the United States at the end of the twentieth century has lost its moral way, many of our voluntary institutions, including our megachurches and our television ministries, have badly let us down.[125]

Indeed, the church has let America – and the world – down. In the words of Ellen G. White,"[t]he piety of the Christian constitutes the standard by which worldlings judge the gospel."[126] American Christianity is often known more for what it is against

---

124 Kramnick and Moore, p. 151.
125 Ibid.
126 Ellen G. White, *Patriarchs and Prophets*, p. 134.

than for its positive attributes. High profile Christians are unfaithful to their spouse, and many Christians hypocritically celebrate political leaders who flaunt the truth and live immoral lives, while condemning the same sins in others. There is no better example of how America has lost its moral way than the current war on truth that we see today. "Fake news" has become the new label we attach to anything we don't agree with, and professed Christians are some of the loudest voices proclaiming fake news.

The prophet Isaiah described our world when he wrote that "justice is driven back, and righteousness stands at a distance; truth has stumbled in the streets, honesty cannot enter. Truth is nowhere to be found, and whoever shuns evil becomes a prey" (Isaiah 59:14–15, NIV).

Jesus especially needs His church to be the salt of the earth and the light of the world in this time of great moral darkness. He needs people who will follow the truth and do justice in this world – people who are not afraid to stand up to racism and oppression. Jesus is looking for people who will live by the golden rule – to do unto others as we would have them do unto us.

What will happen if we do? White put it this way:

> Search heaven and earth, and there is no truth revealed more powerful than that which is made manifest in works of mercy to those who need our sympathy and aid. This is the truth as it is in Jesus. When those who profess the name of Christ shall practice the principles of the golden rule, *the same power will attend the gospel as in apostolic times.*[127]

---

127 Ellen G. White, *Thoughts From the Mount of Blessing*, p. 137, emphasis added.

In this vein of thought, White beautifully described God's last-day message:

The last rays of merciful light, the last message of mercy to be given to the world, is a revelation of His character of love. The children of God are to manifest His glory. In their own life and character they are to reveal what the grace of God has done for them. The light of the Sun of Righteousness is to shine forth in good works – in words of truth and deeds of holiness.[128]

Despite our failures, the Bible foretells a glorious future for God's church. Revelation describes "another angel coming down from heaven. He had great authority, and the earth was illuminated by his splendor" (Revelation 18:1, NIV). If we'll let Him, Jesus will shine through His people during a time of great spiritual darkness to bring hope, love, and truth to those in need:

Arise, shine; for your light has come, and the glory of the Lord has risen upon you. For darkness shall cover the earth, and thick darkness the peoples; but the Lord will arise upon you, and his glory will appear over you. Nations shall come to your light, and kings to the brightness of your dawn (Isaiah 60:1–3, NRSV).

---

128 Ellen G. White, *Christ's Object Lessons,* pp. 415–416.

APPENDIX A

A letter from Ellen G. White to the members of the Woodland Seventh-day Adventist Church.[129]

Oakland, California

July 1880

Dear Brethren and Sisters at Woodland:

I received a letter yesterday from one of your number, Brother Grayson, whom I love and respect as a child of God, nevertheless I was pained by the contents of the letter.

I called for the *Signs* and carefully read Elder Waggoner's article, and reread it. I came to the conclusion if any one of Southern or Northern sentiments could take exceptions to that article, anything they might read in the *Review* or the *Signs* would do them no good. If our pens and voices are to be silent when principles of justice and righteousness in warnings or reproofs [are at stake] because some one or ones, believers or unbelievers, are so sensitive, bigoted and prejudiced, that their peculiar, political sentiments cannot be in any manner referred to, that class will have to be thoroughly converted to God – their sentiments reformed.

---

129 Ellen G. White, *Letter 36*, 1880.

We feel now called upon to speak decidedly. We shall speak and write guardedly, but shall not withhold such matters as are expressed in the *Signs of the Times* to which you make reference.

I have been shown that there were feelings and views with many who profess the faith at Woodland which were not in accordance with the Word of God. The political sentiments and feelings were very strong with some, and this is the reason why they do not grow in grace and the knowledge of the truth. They are offended at any reference to their peculiar sentiments. There has no word of complaint come from any place but Woodland. Not a word, not a feeling has been expressed from Texas or from any of the Southern states. It cannot be that our papers can be printed with no word or reference to anything which will differ from the political sentiments of some. These political sentiments with any one or more believers or unbelievers, if irritated or stirred by such an article as you refer to, I fear will be of no use to us; the less we have of them, the better off we shall be as a people. Every species of slavery is not in accordance with the Word of God. The evils are too great to be enumerated. And if men and women have embraced the solemn truth for these last days that sanctifies the soul, the old political sentiments that sustain the old system of slavery will be, before they are translated, purged from them.

Brother Saunders will change his branch of labor ere long and cannot conscientiously give the sanction to sentiments coming from the office of which he has the control. God's Spirit has been grieved by the feelings cherished by some in the Woodland Church. What these souls need is conversion to God. The light shines so clearly now none need to walk in darkness. My testimonies have gone all through the Southern states. These testimonies speak decidedly and positively in regard to the subject of slavery. It was a system unbalanced and unjust. While we do not and will not dabble in politics, we will be colaborers with Jesus Christ. There are men who possess that spirit of bigotry for instance, the husband of Sister Douglas, who will manifest a rabid spirit, but we must not let these affect us. I tell you no complaint has been made but from Woodland.

Why not cut out of your Bibles, when Christ refers to His work, "The Spirit of the Lord God is upon Me; because He hath anointed Me to preach good tidings unto the meek; he hath sent me to bind up the brokenhearted, to proclaim liberty to the captives, and the opening of the prison to them that are bound" (Isaiah 61:1)?

APPENDIX B

From the appendix in *Patriarchs and Prophets*, authored by the publishers, entitled "On the Question of Theocratic Government."[130]

The question has been raised, and is now much agitated, If a theocracy was good in the time of Israel, why would not a theocratical form of government be equally good for this time? The answer is easy:

A theocracy is a government which derives its power immediately from God. The government of Israel was a true theocracy. That was really a government of God. At the burning bush, God commissioned Moses to lead His people out of Egypt. By signs and wonders and mighty miracles multiplied, God delivered Israel from Egypt and led them through the wilderness and finally into the Promised Land. There He ruled them by judges "until Samuel the prophet," to whom, when he was a child, God spoke, and by whom He made known His will. In the days of Samuel, the people asked that they might have a king. This was allowed, and God chose Saul, and Samuel anointed him king of Israel. Saul failed to do the will of God, and as he rejected the word of the Lord, the Lord rejected him from being king and sent Samuel to anoint David king of Israel; and David's throne God established forevermore. When Solomon succeeded to the kingdom in the place of David his father, the record is: "Then Solomon sat on the throne of the Lord as king instead of David his father." 1 Chronicles 29:23. David's throne was the throne of the Lord, and Solomon sat on the *throne of the Lord* as king over the earthly kingdom of God. The succession to the throne descended in

130 Ellen G. White, *Patriarchs and Prophets*, pp. 761–764.

David's line to Zedekiah, who was made subject to the king of Babylon, and who entered into a solemn covenant before God that he would loyally render allegiance to the king of Babylon. But Zedekiah broke his covenant, and then God said to him:

"Thou, profane wicked prince of Israel, whose day is come, when iniquity shall have an end, thus saith the Lord God; remove the diadem, and take off the crown: This shall not be the same: Exalt him that is low, and abase him that is high. I will overturn, overturn, overturn, it: And it shall be no more, until He come whose right it is; and I will give it Him." Ezekiel 21:25–27. See also chapter 17:1–21.

The kingdom was then subject to Babylon. When Babylon fell, and Medo-Persia succeeded, it was overturned the first time. When Medo-Persia fell and was succeeded by Greece, it was overturned the second time. When the Greek empire gave way to Rome, it was overturned the third time. And then says the word, "It shall be no more, until He come whose right it is; and I will give it Him." Who is He whose right it is? "Thou . . . shalt call His name Jesus. He shall be great, and shall be called the Son of the Highest: and the Lord God shall give unto Him the throne of His father David: and He shall reign over the house of Jacob forever; and of His kingdom there shall be no end." Luke 1:31–33. And while He was here as "that Prophet," a Man of Sorrows and acquainted with grief, the night in which He was betrayed, He Himself declared, "My kingdom is not of this world." Thus, the throne of the Lord has been removed from this world and will "be no more, until He come whose right it is," and then it will be given Him. And *that time* is the end of this world, and the beginning of "the world to come."

To the twelve apostles the Saviour said, "I appoint unto you a kingdom, as My Father hath appointed unto Me; that ye may eat and drink at My table in My kingdom, and sit on thrones, judging the twelve tribes of Israel." Luke 22:29, 30. From Matthew's account of Christ's promise to the twelve, we learn when it will be fulfilled; "in the regeneration when the Son of Man shall sit in the throne of His glory, ye also shall sit upon twelve thrones, judging the twelve tribes of Israel." Matthew 19:28. In the parable of the talents, Christ represents Himself under the figure of a nobleman who "went into a far country to receive for himself a kingdom, and to return." Luke 19:12. And He Himself has told us when He will sit upon the throne of His glory: "When the Son of man shall come in His glory, and all the holy angels with Him, *then* shall He sit upon the throne of His glory: and before Him shall be gathered all nations." Matthew 25:31, 32.

To this time, the revelator looks forward when he says, "The kingdoms of this world *are become* the kingdoms of our Lord, and of His Christ; and He shall reign forever and ever." Revelation 11:15. The context clearly shows when this will take place: "the nations were angry, and Thy wrath is come, and the time of the dead, that they should be judged, and that Thou shouldest give reward unto Thy servants the prophets, and to the saints, and them that fear Thy name, small and great; and shouldest destroy them which destroy the earth." Verse 18. It is at the time of the final judgment, the reward of the righteous, and the punishment of the wicked that the kingdom of Christ will be set up. When all who oppose the sovereignty of Christ have been destroyed, the kingdoms of this world become the kingdoms of our Lord and of His Christ.

Then Christ will reign, "King of kings, and Lord of lords." Revelation 19:16. "And the kingdom and dominion, and the greatness of the kingdom under the whole heaven, shall be given to the people of the saints of the Most High." And "the saints of the Most High shall take the kingdom, and possess the kingdom forever, even forever and ever." Daniel 7:27, 18.

Until that time, the kingdom of Christ cannot be established on the earth. His kingdom is not of this world. His followers are to account themselves "strangers and pilgrims on the earth." Paul says, "Our citizenship is in heaven; from whence also we wait for a Saviour, the Lord Jesus Christ." Hebrews 11:13; Philippians 3:20, R.V.

Since the kingdom of Israel passed away, God has never delegated authority to any man or body of men to execute His laws as such. "Vengeance is mine; I will repay, saith the Lord." Romans 12:19. Civil governments have to do with the relations of man with man, but they have nothing whatever to do with the duties that grow out of man's relation to God.

Except the kingdom of Israel, no government has ever existed on the earth in which God by inspired men directed the affairs of state. Whenever men have endeavored to form such a government as that of Israel, they have, of necessity, taken it upon themselves to interpret and enforce the law of God. They have assumed the right to control the conscience and thus have usurped the prerogative of God.

In the former dispensation, while sins against God were visited with temporal penalties, the judgments executed were not only by divine sanction but also under His direct control, and by His command. Sorcerers were to be put to death. Idolaters were to be slain. Profanity and sacrilege were punished with death. Whole nations of idolaters were to be exterminated. But the infliction of these penalties was directed by Him who reads the hearts of men, who knows the measure of their guilt, and who deals with His creatures in wisdom and mercy. When men, with human frailties and passions, undertake to do this work, it needs no argument to show that the door is opened to unrestrained injustice and cruelty. The most inhuman crimes will be perpetrated, and all in the sacred name of Christ.

From the laws of Israel, which punished offenses against God, arguments have been drawn to prove the duty of punishing similar sins in this age. All persecutors have employed them to justify their deeds. The principle that God has delegated to human authority the right to control the conscience is the very foundation of religious tyranny and persecution. But all who reason thus lose sight of the fact that we are now living in a different dispensation, under conditions wholly different from those of Israel; that the kingdom of Israel was a type of the kingdom of Christ, which will not be set up until His second coming; and that the duties that pertain to man's relation to God are not to be regulated or enforced by human authority.